SECRET
PANDEMIC

SECRET PANDEMIC

THE SEARCH FOR CONNECTION IN A LONELY WORLD

SIMONE HENG

LIONCREST
PUBLISHING

SECRET PANDEMIC

The Search for Connection in a Lonely World

ISBN   978-1-5445-2759-8   *Hardcover*

978-1-5445-2757-4   *Paperback*

978-1-5445-2758-1   *Ebook*

For my parents, Robert and Sandra.
I know you did the best you could with what you had at the time.
You were both human connection superheroes in your own way.

CONTENTS

INTRODUCTION

My hand is shaking. I cannot take down the TikTok video. I cannot even toggle to the trash bin icon. I have been found out. I am flushed red and mortified. Shame floods my body. I have put up a video about the first time I learned to say "sorry." The story is about my upbringing in an Asian household where the word "sorry" wasn't used. The point of the video is that I was already nineteen when I learned to say "sorry" without sarcasm—that we can learn from unlikely teachers how to become better. The story is meant to be inspirational. It is, until my past comes back to bite me. *I am a fraud*, I think. I have been found out.

A young man writes in my video comments, "I served you at my store in 2015. You shouted at me. You were the worst customer I had in six years." I toggle quickly to find his name and add him on Instagram, where I can message him voice notes to apologize. I delete the video, hands trembling. I want to shrink so small that I disappear. The shame that washes over me and sinks into my veins is like ink dropped in water; it spreads quickly, pervasively. My unlovable past is back to haunt me. For a moment, I am that girl whose cousin made a group chat on WhatsApp to bitch about her on a bachelorette party. For a moment, I am the girl who never had a pack of friends at high school. For a moment, I am the girl who didn't even know herself, so her colleagues could not stand her. I am the girl who didn't know how to love because she wasn't shown enough love.

I stop myself. My counselor told me that catastrophizing is part of a trauma response. I breathe. I remember all the self-work and research I have done on connection; my hand stops trembling. I send a voice note to the young man, and I apologize. As I do this, my mind says, "You were the worst kind of shitty, enraged person." Then my rational brain kicks in and says, "You *were* that person. That person was born in the belly of grief and loneliness. You do better now. GO FIX THIS."

After counseling myself, I can dialogue with the young man. He watches some of my speeches, and I send him screenshots of messages from service people from when I lived in Dubai, who got promoted because I told their managers how amazing they were. I am trying to prove that the trauma that filled me with rage was a moment in time, my actions were not my character, and they certainly had nothing to do with him. He forgives me. He tells me I am so strong to have gone through what I have. Although he forgives me, it takes me weeks until I forgive myself. I am glad he got in touch; it was a mirror held up to me in the midst of writing this book, reminding me of the human part of "human connection." To be human is to be deeply fallible.

You may feel rich with rage. Your trauma is bigger than you. You look at others with envy of the ease with which they view the world. People for them are not a threat. They feel so safe. You can tell by just looking at them. You have not felt safe in years. They laugh open-mouthed at criticism, and it cascades off them like water off the proverbial duck's back. For you, criticism is a deep trigger, like a thorn being ripped out of the flesh of your foot. Like me, the lack of safety could have started by not being soothed by a caregiver or by losing a direct family member young.

By the time my mother's legs stopped working, I felt even less safe. We were not one of the chosen families where the father bounces back and survives cancer. We were not one of the chosen families whose mother walks again after a stroke.

I remember when I started very delayed grief therapy. I had disassociated from my unbearable pain, so it was almost two decades later when I finally got to a therapist's office. But better late than never. In therapy, I learned I needed help, not just to grieve my father's death or my mother's paralysis, but I needed to heal parts of me born much earlier, in my childhood.

My therapist asked me, "What do you want to get out of this?"

I said with self-hatred mixed with envy, "I want to be one of those easygoing people. Those people who are carefree and for whom everything is water off a duck's back."

Like the Aussie customers I had once watched at my father's shop, replying "Can't complain" to the question, "How are you?" So laid back, their gratitude so entrenched, or their expectations so small it could be summed up in two words.

I sat in that counselor's office, in my socks, cross-legged on a chair. My arms crossed around me, embracing myself for fear that I would fall apart. I thought, *Who were those people?* Those people seemed to live on another planet foreign to us "trauma babies," people for whom dysfunction was an ever-present shadow in our childhood. *We would never be allowed entry into a smooth, easy existence,* I thought to myself. But that statement, you will learn through this book, just wasn't true. I secretly knew that it was untrue; otherwise, why would I have walked to reception and booked my next session? I had

a small sliver of hope embedded in my gut after that session.
I did not know it yet, but that sliver was human connection.

Have you felt a hint of disconnection from yourself? You
remember your joy as a child. Carefree, artistic, and loving.
Somewhere, a relative or primary caregiver puts you down.
They do it again and again daily. For those of us who experience it, it is called a "little t" trauma, a chipping away at who
you are. We talk too loudly, so we are shushed. We gain weight,
so we are publicly shamed. We don't get the best grades, so
we're destined to be the "dumb one" in the family.

I hope this book will be your first insight into the fact you
are not alone. I will speak about things that are felt universally:
loneliness in the midst of unprecedented digital connectivity,
deepening sadness at the lack of human connection caused by
an isolating pandemic, and the effects of childhood trauma
on how we connect with others. I'll also pull back the curtain
to discuss things that some of us from an Asian background
do not say out loud, let alone write in print. Maybe this will
stop you from feeling you have something to be ashamed of
because nothing augments shame like silence.

My hope is that you will feel less alone after reading this
book. A book on human connection that doesn't just talk
about it but makes you feel more connected. Like your hopes
for a life released from being "unlovable" exists. I know it exists
because I have emerged on the other side. I started my healing by reading books and talking to people, tears streaming
down my face like a forgotten pot on the stove boiling over.
Bubbling with pain in my gut. I could not keep my lid on any
longer. This book is designed to point an arrow at the places
in your life where love and connection could flow in and fill
the gaps. Then I hope it urges you to find other resources, like
therapy or a coach, to build yourself back up with a more
bespoke approach.

Through this book, you will learn how to reconnect with yourself. You'll start thinking about why you feel a certain way when you fight with your partner, the tendrils of the argument reaching far back into your past. You'll know who to go to when it's time to speak about your pain. You'll understand the kind of trust that is the foundation for authentic connection. You'll find ways you never thought of to reach out to stop the chill of loneliness setting into your bones. At the end of each chapter, there will be practical connection challenges that can guide you in taking action. We all need to step beyond the pages to form relationships, and these will show you how to build rapport in your communication.

I could give you my professional bio here and tell you that I speak on stages around the world on the power of human connection. And that I have worked frontline for some of the biggest broadcasters. But as we already know, none of those things made me a master at human connection. None of those achievements healed me. In reality, your achievements won't heal you either. The media taught me to communicate, but it didn't help me build the kind of connection I'd want to share in a book.

I think what is more important to note is the bio between the lines. As I know it is for many, a search for love and connection is the thread running throughout my entire life story.

I was born in Singapore and raised in Australia to immigrant parents. My childhood was emotionally exhausting, and as soon as I could, I put space between myself and the place I was raised. I used ambition and achievement to get me out of there. Beginning with a scholarship to Switzerland at seventeen, I learned for the first time after living with three families that shouting and walking on eggshells were not an experience all children had.

I now have a Cavalier King Charles spaniel called Charlie;

she is the worst at saving face ever. She wags her tail with a desperation and neediness for cuddles that stops people on the street. "Look at her tail; it's so cute." *She's so obvious,* they think and point. Her whole bum moves when she wags her tail, impeding how she walks. All because she wants love and approval. That was me. My entire way of connecting with people was impaired because I believed I was completely starved of the true connection we all need. This gave off a desperation in the way I connected with others, which was noticeable to everyone but me. This desperate energy repelled the connection I wanted so badly even further. This book traces the journey into how that behavior came to be in the hope that those who see themselves in my story will find healing and connection.

Rather than tell you I am a master, I wanted to open this book by telling you how I have failed deeply as a human connector. At one point or another, I may have failed in every way you can imagine, but I keep getting back up again and hope to get better at it. I hope my devotion to being better at it makes you see you can do the same. Eventually, as the chapters develop, you'll see that it isn't optional. Through this book, you'll learn that human connection is integral to our physical and mental well-being, and there will be many studies and experts cited to support that.

I sit here now from a place of hard-won healing and a deep self-awareness that the learning never stops. I can look in the mirror and comfortably say, "I like me." I have beautiful friends, a wonderful partner, a purpose, a mission, and, most importantly, wonderful relationships with my remaining direct family members. Those connections are something I needed to feel I could write this book from a place of resolve.

This book is not didactic, and it is not highly prescriptive. As Brené Brown implies in *The Gifts of Imperfection,* I am not a "how to" kind of girl. I am not here to give you three hacks to connect with people or tell you how to use mentalist body language techniques to control peoples' minds. The practical parts of this book are more observances and suggestions than they are top tips. This is also because my concerns around loneliness are ever-morphing with our changing world. Further, be it from a pandemic or increased digitization, our needs for connection will change constantly. Consequently, this book was designed to walk the talk on connection. That you would feel less alone, different, and lacking in belonging, simply in the act of reading it.

I'm Simone. Let's *connect*.

CHAPTER 1

KILLING US SOFTLY

The Secret Loneliness Pandemic

S elf-connection is defined by Tim Sitt, a child and family therapist and registered social worker, as "the process of being in touch with the worthiness and wholeness of your Self regardless of the form of experience you are having. These forms could be feelings, thoughts, expectations, beliefs, or attitudes."[1] Without self-connection, effectively knowing ourselves deeply and intimately, we cannot connect well with others. Instead, we send an avatar of ourselves into the world, and people connect not with us authentically but with behaviors born of our triggers and the lingering remnants of our trauma. In our increasingly busy and digitally distracted lives, it becomes easy to avoid the work of getting to know ourselves better, and that means stunting our ability to connect well with others.

The 2018 Cigna Loneliness Index surveyed twenty thousand Americans and discovered that loneliness had reached "epidemic" proportions, with almost half of participants registering as feeling "always" or "sometimes" alone.[2] In 2018, Britain appointed its first "minister for loneliness," who is charged with tackling what former Prime Minister Theresa May called the "sad reality of modern life." As you will read throughout this book, a lack of human connection can lead to many different issues that you may not immediately link. Hoarding. Rage. Addiction. Depression.[3] And because of the shame associated with saying "I'm lonely," we've been suffering silently for a lot longer than anyone wants to admit.

THE PANDEMIC OF LONELINESS

In 2003, I stood watching my father give the eulogy at my Chinese grandmother's funeral. I had just returned to Australia from studying in Switzerland for a year, and as a family, we had made the trip to Singapore. My father had been away, a migrant in another country, for almost twenty years. His relationship with my Teochew grandmother consisted of only peppered phone calls with months in between, a tenuous link at best. Regardless, he had to give the eulogy because he was the eldest son in a Chinese family and that is what they did.

I stood watching my father speak, his slight paunch encased in a white polo shirt like ripe Christmas pudding. I observed his humbled demeanor, always head bowed, facing the mole on his arm that had been getting darker from golf. He had only recently started taking one weekend day off each week from work at his news agency. He still didn't even know how to use sunscreen; that's how little of a break he ever took. He would come home from golf with arms like Cadbury top deck chocolate, white beneath his capped sleeves and deep brown on his forearms, then apply sunscreen, like an after-sun aloe vera treatment. Gosh, that made me and my sister giggle.

My eyes became blurry as I shifted focus from his tanned forearms to his kind eyes. I heard the sound of his voice paying tribute to a grandmother I barely knew and did not speak the same language as. I was out of my own body. A dangerous thought flashed in my mind like rogue lightning in a summer sky. I thought to myself, *Oh my gosh, I will have to do this for my father one day. I will have to get up at his funeral and grieve him and say all kinds of nice things about him in the past tense, and I never want that day to come.* Little did I know, exactly one year later, I would be up there, on a pulpit, in a church, surrounded by a sea of sobs, paying premature tribute to Robert Heng.

Because at that very moment, as he was speaking, eulogizing my grandmother, a cancer was growing inside him. A cancer which, by the time we found it, would overwhelm his small body and kill him. It would be so painful that they would have to infuse him with morphine like I infuse my morning tea with chamomile. Fast, strong, and so pervasive that his color would change to jaundiced yellow like the hot water in my tea. It wasn't like global warming. Here there were no warning signs. It just happened, and our world ended.

Like the cancer growing in my father, there is a cancer secretly growing in the body of the human race. It is not COVID-19, and it isn't global warming. It is a cancer that poses huge threats to our mental and physical health and our entire way of functioning as a species. It's surrounded by shame and whispered about in communities, and it befuddles TikTok-using teens with high anxiety. It exists behind keyboards and messenger texts, between friends on social media.

This secret illness is a pandemic of its own, and it is the pandemic of loneliness. The ill effects of loneliness have long been well-supported by research. According to one meta-analysis, a lack of social connection heightens health risks as much as smoking fifteen cigarettes a day or having an alcohol use disorder. Loneliness and social isolation are twice as harmful to physical and mental health as obesity. Even sadder is that it has taken a contagious virus for us to see how badly a lack of human connection affects us because, like the cancer inside my dad, it has been killing us softly long before we had a clue.

DEFINING HUMAN CONNECTION

What is human connection? What is this term so often thrown around but seemingly intangible? It is so much easier to explain why we need it than what it is. From my conversations with digitally reared teens, I think knowing how to define it may be vital for Gen Z, who came up as the loneliest of all generations in the Cigna Loneliness Index. How do we know when we are making, or are in the presence of, a genuine human connection?

We have all experienced that moment where, when we meet someone for the first time, we are on the exact same wavelength. Our opinions, morals, values, and worldviews are in sync. We see so much of ourselves in that person that energy starts to spark off as the conversation flows and flows, and by the end of the meeting, pandemic or not, we are inspired to hug, shake hands, or in some way physically touch our new friend. The connection feels right in our gut. It feels almost safe for us to disclose our vulnerabilities to this new person because we see so much of them in ourselves. I think we can agree that these connections feel distinctly different from shallow conversations shared over drinks at some business networking event. Finding new authentic connections can sometimes feel like walking around a barren desert and stumbling upon a member of your party that you have been stranded from!

By surveying people online, I got some incredible definitions, and they are worth featuring because of certain trends that recur. Here are some of my favorites:

- "No one lives or is meant to live on their own. For me, this is powerful and humbling because it gives everyone a clue that we're all bound in a deeper sense."

- "Human connection is the transfer of message, thought, or emotion to another."

- "Human connection, to me, is the sharing or exchange of experience, either through emotions or messages."

- "We might not see eye to eye, but the ability to connect to something beyond ourselves is an intrinsic part of being human."

- "The experience of feeling close and connected to others. It involves feeling loved, cared for, and valued."

- "Human connection is about communicating with another person heart to heart. Without heart, there is no human connection!"

- "Human connection is communication between one another."

- "Soulful conversations."

- "To me, human connection is when a human actively listens to understand and empathize with another human's existence, truth, and situation."

- "Understanding each other."

- "Human connection is touch."

- "Deep interconnection of the mind, heart, and soul."

- "It's the bond we make with other people."

- "Human connection is an energy exchange between people who are paying attention to one another. It has the power to deepen the moment, inspire change, and build trust."

- "Vulnerability."

- "It means, for me, a sense of belonging."

- "When two people can relate to each other through their commonalities and want to continue relating to each other despite their differences."

- "Human connection is showing empathy, compassion, kindness, and lifting one another despite differences. Great understanding and acceptance of different views."

- "Human connection to me is our ability to share emotion, to relate to others, to rely on others, and to be relied upon by others."

- "To go beyond the surface and have a heart-to-heart talk. Things that matter to our soul and heart. Of what hurts, what breaks, what lifts, what needs, what matters."

My personal definition of human connection? It is the natural energetic rapport we experience with another human when we are able to see, feel, and discover ourselves mirrored in them.

WIRED FOR CONNECTION

For me to really explain the extent to which we need human connection, we have to turn back the clock to our days in prehistoric tribes. Like most aspects of the way our brains are wired, our innate need for human connection happened when we were still in hunter-gatherer societies, running away from saber-toothed tigers. Everything about the way we operated during this time was wired to keep us safe. If we were pregnant and could not gather food for our family, the other tribeswomen would share their harvest with us. If we were injured and couldn't keep up with the rest of the hunt, the other tribesmen would hunt game to feed our families. And at night, when we settled down to sleep around that fire, the other tribespeople would take turns keeping watch for predators while we slept. In fact, evidence suggests that people in the past devoted significant time and scarce resources to caring for those in need. As far back as the Neanderthals, humans have cared for their weak and sick.[4] We realized there was safety in numbers, and at our core, we are still tribal creatures who crave connection. We need to have human connection, and when we are disconnected from the tribe, some really dark and scary things can start to happen.

DEFINING DISCONNECTION

Interestingly, the antithesis of human connection, disconnection, is a much easier term to define. I think that could be a marker that we all have tasted disconnection; it's palpable. Oxford's Lexico.com defines disconnection as "the state of being isolated or detached." This is a term that will come up again and again in this book. Disconnection. Detachment. Isolation. They are all very dangerous for human beings. Johann Hari, author of *Lost Connections*, defines disconnection as being "cut off from something we innately need but seem to have lost along the way."[5]

Our brains imprint the feeling of that discomfort strongly for us in the hope we avoid it and stay with our tribe at all costs.

In his book, *Social*, Matthew D. Lieberman further explains that the pain of disconnection we experience when we are cast out of the tribe has enabled our survival as a species. It's also led to our dominance and enabled humans to thrive: "By activating the same neural circuitry that causes physical pain, our experience of social pain helps ensure the survival of our children by helping keep them close to their parents."[6]

In a modern world, where we don't live in tribes that we can be cast out of, how do we know when we are disconnected? The red flag of disconnection can start with our sleep. Without that person keeping watch over the tribe, on your own, cast out, you would have to rouse many times in the night to look out for predators yourself. According to Dr. Louise Hawkley from the University of Chicago, people who feel lonely will have reduced quality of sleep and experience what is called "micro awakenings." Like an amputee missing a phantom leg, your brain is missing the tribe it was meant to be attached to.[7] These micro awakenings are used to study how lonely people are. When I was serving two weeks' quarantine in Perth, Australia, my mental health calls to my hotel room would always include: "How are you feeling? How are you sleeping?" for this very reason. If you experienced less than good sleep during COVID-19, you are not alone, and disconnection could well be why.

To help you identify the different rungs of connection, we need to be fully connected socially. Looking at the work of Bruce A. Austin at Rochester University of Technology could help. He shares that there are three different categories of loneliness: intimate loneliness (a yearning for an intimate partner), relational loneliness (a yearning for close family and friends), and collective loneliness (a yearning for a group that shares your same purpose).[8]

We'll revisit these concepts in the following chapters, but

here's how profound loneliness showed up in my life in 2014. After ten years abroad with ample friends and creatives who shared my mission, I returned to Perth to care for my mom, who had become disabled. I had none of these three orbits of connection. It was the loneliest I have ever been. My family relationships, which were already strained, were stretched as thin as fishing line because of Mom's condition. These stressors actually caused me memory loss; allow me to me explain.

HOW LONELINESS AFFECTS THE BRAIN

During this time, I had gotten a short-term contract at a local radio station as an announcer. I had an afternoon show and would play music and run the station competitions. I remember one week where I ran a contest and completely forgot that I had just run it. I would forget to write down the winner and which song I ran the contest after. My memory, which had always been stellar, was disappearing. I was horrified. I started wondering what was going wrong with me. Did I have the same degenerative disease that gave my mom dementia at sixty-five and put her in a wheelchair? A disease so rare, with so little known about it, that in the private Facebook group for it, users share terrifying symptoms like: "Does anyone else here get terrible night sweats and incontinence?"

One night a few weeks later, it all came to a head. There is a button that every radio station in the world has. They call it different things depending on what market you are in, but basically, a push of this button puts the entire radio station into automation mode while everyone at home sleeps and keeps the music playing. I had been so stressed by what was happening with Mom that I jumped in the car after my shift and drove to meet my cousin for an evening movie. All of a sudden, there was silence from the radio station as I drove along the freeway. It was dark outside, the sun having just gone down; I felt and heard the gravel squelch under my tires as I pulled over to really hear. I felt like every person on the road around me, sitting in their cars, was jamming and toggling their radio knobs, wondering why there was silence on their favorite Perth radio station for the first time in thirty years.

DEAD AIR.

Dead air is the nightmare of radio broadcasters globally. As I pulled over on the side of the highway, I could hear a silent howling scream of shame from anyone who had ever taught me my craft. I remember scrunching my forehead and trying to think over and over, "Did I put the station in automation? Did I press the button?" Was this really DEAD air silence, or was this just *my* old car and *my* radio? My boss rang me shortly after and, being one of the better managers I ever had, she kindly told me it could not happen again. I was mortified. An engineer dialed in remotely and put the station back on air.

What was happening to me? I finally went to see my local doctor after this incident to find out what was happening to my memory. The doctor called in a psychiatrist. He said, "Simone, do you know when people are in a car crash, they can't remember what has happened?"

I replied, "Yes, that's shock!"

"You're experiencing a little bit of that," he said. "All these things going through your life, your mom having a stroke, her paralysis, your family members ostracizing you, lack of friendships. These things have you in fight-or-flight mode."

I was so confused. You see, I didn't know what stress actually WAS. This was 2014; the world was not yet having these discussions about mental health. I did not know that it came from a biological response.[9] I just blamed myself over and over for being an unlikeable, high-strung person.

I also had ignorantly assumed moving to one of the world's

most isolated capital cities, where the pace was slow and the media industry sparse, would rid me of the stress I had experienced living as an expat in bustling cities like Dubai and Singapore. I equated slower lifestyles with less stress because I knew so little about what stress was. I never realized that my stress response systems had become altered from early on in my childhood by not having my needs for love and affection met. In short, I had no idea stress was linked to a lack of human connection.

Let me explain how a fight-or-flight response is connected to a lack of social belonging. Come back with me to the cave where we were hunter-gatherers again and imagine how, when we were separated from the tribe, our body experienced a fight-or-flight response to the lack of safety. Our body was flooded with stress hormones like cortisol. This is okay on an incidental level; it's akin to an alarm telling you to go out and connect. The problem is now, in the way we live, more digitally connected than ever but simultaneously lonelier than ever, many of us can stay in fight-or-flight mode chronically. This means those stress hormones are flooding us constantly, damaging our immunity, and leading to many life-shortening diseases. Rigorous epidemiological studies have linked loneliness and social isolation to heart disease, cancer, depression, diabetes, and suicide.[10] The lonely brain sleeps less and is on edge in its hypervigilance against threats and is anxious. This chronically being in fight-or-flight mode means that lonely people are more likely to die prematurely than those with strong social connections.

THE IMPORTANCE OF HUMAN CONNECTION

There's another reason I really want to emphasize how pivotal the role human connection is in achieving the kind of life you desire. There is a very well-known motivational theory in psychology by Abraham Maslow. Maslow's Hierarchy of Needs is illustrated in a pyramid; it lists the qualities human beings need to reach the height of their potential or "self-actualization."[11]

Maslow created the model by studying what he believed were the top 1 percent of the college population, people he believed were thriving.

So, what has this got to do with human connection? At the bottom of the pyramid, there are our physiological needs like food, water, and shelter, followed by our safety needs like psychological safety, health, and employment. Just above that is belonging and love. Without friendships and intimate relationships, we do not move higher up the pyramid. We cannot get to the next level of esteem or our final full potential or self-actualization.

Now we know that human connection and a sense of belonging can help us become our best selves. We know that we can experience a shorter life span and be stressed all the time without it. But what if the very reason we have to keep away from other humans is to protect us from a virus, and yet the very act of separation causes us to erode the very immunity we need? The irony is not lost on me.

THE PANDEMIC HAS CAUSED MORE LONELINESS

Enter the coronavirus. No book on connection can ever be written again without a mention of the COVID-19 pandemic. The world was already suffering a loneliness epidemic, and then our ability to touch was taken away from us.

Neuroscientist and clinical psychologist James Coan explains what happens in the biological response to disconnection:

Well, one of the things I worry most about is that, when you are overtaxed in this way, by involuntary isolation, one of the regions of the brain that is going to be fatigued or slowly disinvested in, is your prefrontal cortex, your ability to think abstractly, plan contingencies that make sense, et cetera. In effect you get dumber, right when we should not get dumber. That's one of the things we can expect from long periods of social isolation. One of the symptoms of depression is cognitive difficulties, problems with memory and so forth. This is the sort of thing we can expect from social isolation as well.

What COVID-19 has done is push people who were not feeling part of the tribe so close to the edge that they have jumped off the proverbial cliff. In April 2020, my close friend and beloved mentor took his life in a Melbourne quarantine facility. My eyes tear up just writing this because if I could tell you how loved this person was, it's almost inconceivable he could not himself see his own virtues. He had left Dubai to repatriate back to Australia and had left a marriage and an industry behind. The feeling of isolation is so large and so insurmountable that many would rather be swallowed by it. Some call this darkness loneliness; some call it depression. What I know for sure is that human connection is the rope we can fling into it and allow someone we love dearly to pull themselves out. I wish I had done that for him; I wish I knew what was happening at that time.

The loneliness crisis we are experiencing was happening before COVID-19. I know because I was speaking on it before the pandemic, but the virus has shone a huge spotlight on something we knew was already under threat. Now, if we don't do something about it, it's just killing us loudly instead of softly.

Try the following connection challenges to practice actual connection, so we don't just read and talk about it.

REACH OUT TO THOSE YOU HAVEN'T SPOKEN TO IN A WHILE.

Look through your phone's most used messaging app. Find three people who you have not spoken to in six months or longer. Look specifically for people in your circle who may withdraw and tend to self-isolate. First, text them, wait for the text response, and then leave a voice note as a reply. If they reciprocate with a voice note, listen and connect with their voice note. Do they sound okay? Escalate the exchange using a phone call or video. Remember, the best digital connection leads to an in-person connection (more on that in Chapter 10), so create time to meet in person for a catch-up.

PICK UP THE PHONE AND CALL SOMEONE INSTEAD OF A VIDEO CALL.

A recent study by Jeffery A. Hall, Natalie Pennington, and Amanda J. Holstrom on connecting through technology during COVID-19 revealed that Zoom fatigue is real. As a result of its ubiquity, people now associate video calls as stressful and anxiety-inducing, making them feel even lonelier. The "old school" phone call has thus made a return.[12] Understand that the smile is to the mouth what eye contact is to the face. So, smile when on that call so that anyone you love at risk on the other end can hear your warmth.

CHAPTER 2

VULNERABILITY

The Gift of Loss and Grief

M y phone is flashing. I put down the black handheld microphone. I am standing in the world's biggest mall, and the fluorescent lights in the Du store are blinding. I've just finished hosting a radio roadshow. The day before, I had been in Switzerland, seeing my best friends from my time there as an exchange student. We sat at Fischer's Fritz, a stunning outdoor eatery on the banks of the Zürichsee and ate buttery Zopf bread discussing my mom. The girls had stayed with us for three months in Australia, shortly after my dad had died, almost a decade before. They knew my mother well. They asked me how she was. I replied, for some reason tearing up, "She's been getting worse and worse. The house is in chaos. She gets mad. I know if I get a call, it will be my turn to go back there. My sister has done enough." My voice cracks the way it does for so many of us when we articulate a deep fear we have thought about for ages but never uttered.

Now back in Dubai, twenty-four hours later, the phone flashes from a private number. Somehow my intuition tells me it's my sister. Hadn't I felt this before, this impending doom, with my father when I imagined eulogizing him? I knew this call was coming. My sister says, "Simone, Mum's had a stroke. If I were you, I'd want to come home."

I know this tone of voice. In our family, this is muscle memory…

THE NEWS THAT TAKES YOUR BREATH AWAY

When I was nineteen, I was working part-time at a sports store at the local mall. My father had been in the hospital for some months, but my parents had decided to keep from us what was really going on until they had confirmation. I would like to think they were on the brink of telling us when a familiar face walked into the store. It was the nurse from the hospital treating Dad. She had a kind, well-intentioned face like the favorite mom of all your high school friends. We talked about the weather, and then she asked me how I was and how my father was.

"He's okay, just lashing out somewhat, which is quite out of character," I said.

"Yes, it's like that when they have cancer," she replied, a well-worn sadness curling her bottom lip and furrowing her brow.

I didn't even know. I had suspected Dad had cancer, but at that moment, I hadn't heard it from my parents' mouths. I remember running off the shop floor and sobbing in the back room, surrounded by bricks of orange Nike shoeboxes, which I felt were caving in on me. Ninety days later, my father died.

I still remember the evening he passed. The Silver Chain nurse came to the house. We were told it was time. My father's hospital bed had been placed in my bedroom because it was on the ground floor of the house. My mother, sister, and I, along with my mother's brother, surrounded the thin remnants of what was left of my father. His fragility was protected in the duvet like a bird I once rescued and padded in tissues for its comfort. I clutched his hand. He was barely breathing. My mother was keening, a kind of wailing that chilled me to the bone. Her body rocking back and forth. I had only ever seen women in documentaries behaving like this after losing their babies in famine. My mother of steel was devoured without him. She melted down that evening.

My uncle shook his head repeatedly, saying, "Robbie, don't go. Don't go." Dad exhaled, his eyes rolled backward, and then...he was gone. It is surreal to see someone die in front of you. When my then-nineteen-year-old self had watched movies, seeing an actor take their last breath was dramatic, but there was always a distance. Something about knowing that the person who is dying is acting made the experience sanitized. It certainly never prepared me to see the person I loved most in the world take their last breath. Those of us who have seen someone pass are connected in that most intimate of moments.

I slept that night in my sister's room. I couldn't sleep in my room with his body there. The next morning, I went to the bed he was in and looked at him with a strange distance. Touched his cold hand. It looked like his hand, with the mole on it I had come to know for years. But he was thin and gray and empty. The body was just a sack of flesh. What we hear about the soul bringing the body to life is absolutely true. The soul animates. Death in that moment looked so final to me. There was nothing in the world that could be done to breathe life back into my father. What I saw was just the carcass, riddled with cancer. Huge bruises on his back when we turned his body over to get him ready for the morgue. I later learned this was postmortem lividity, where the pooling of blood after death takes on a blue-and-black marbled appearance. I had never felt more like a child than in that moment. Why had no one prepared me for this? Why did no one protect me? It looked like he had been assaulted. Maybe in a way, he had.

In the days that followed, I helped my sister organize the funeral booklet. Relatives streamed into our home. My sister held it together. My mother, sobbing constantly, was told by old Asian aunties who were not qualified to counsel those who are grieving, "Be strong. Don't cry." I saw her push the natural reaction she was meant to have deep inside her. Isn't this how my dad had gotten cancer in the first place? By pushing all of his trauma deep inside until his dis-ease became disease. I tried to do what they said because, at that time, I was conditioned by my culture to treat anyone older than me as wiser, as someone I should respect because "they know more about life than I do." Life has now taught me otherwise. Just because people are older doesn't mean they know more about good mental health than you do. Pushing down my grief almost destroyed me.

We picked up my father's sisters from the airport. They had flown in from Singapore. I had to tell them Dad had passed. The first thing one of them said to my puffy-eyed face was, "Y'all didn't pray hard enough." As recently converted charismatic Christians, this was their belief. There was very little comfort or acknowledgment of how I felt, just more disconnection. The days prepping for the funeral were so stressful I wanted to run away. My father and I had been best friends. I didn't see the point of being at home any longer with this family I loved but did not really like, let alone felt I belonged to. Now I realize this internal unrest, this seeming contradiction of feelings, was the beginning of my developing my own precious voice, which would become a powerful gift in my life. Your voice is powerful too. This was also actually the beginning of my self-connection. It felt just like a budding inside of me. The beginning of valuing my own opinion away from the smothering obedience and obligation that comes with being an Asian girl in an Asian family.

THE FUNERAL

On the day of the funeral, I watched my mother walk in front of the hearse early in the morning. We walked ahead in front of her. I will never forget seeing her like that, crumpled over, keening like a wild animal shot in the leg, yet still somehow keeping her feet in motion. Life had hunted her. *What form of my mother will emerge after this?* I wondered. *Would she become hardened and stronger, or would she soften and finally show up as the affectionate mother I longed for?*

We got into the hearse and drove to Riverton, where my father had worked at his shop for almost thirty years. If I close my eyes now, I can still feel the excitement of arriving there with Mom as a child after a hot summer primary school day and seeing him behind the counter, dutifully serving someone. I would jump up and down to show him I was there, the countertop otherwise concealing my presence. The minute his customers left, I would run and hug him. Sometimes he would hand me an ice-cold Coke as a treat from the mini-fridge. My father, to this day, was the most physically and verbally affectionate Chinese Singaporean person I have ever met. In the months that would come after his death, every time I had to drive past his shop, my heart would palpitate, having to reconcile that he no longer existed. Another man behind that counter, running the shop like a mistaken alternate reality.

We entered the church, our local parish. My father had adopted Catholicism for my mom when they married. I remember him snoring away in church in the nineties, but in the months before he died, he had actually drawn a lot of comfort from the religion, and I am happy he did. I walked behind the coffin. I had pulled my hair around my face to avoid being judged for how I was expressing my grief. I was called up to eulogize him. To talk to people about the kind of man he was, and when I looked up, vision blurred with tears, I saw a sea of people. Literally, people streaming out into the church's grassy courtyard with Perth's autumn light unwrapping itself on their shoulders. My breath caught in my throat. How many people had shown up for this humble shopkeeper? Decades later, I would be confronted in Singapore by a British man who claimed that it's ridiculous to think you can make a difference in this life. I did not have the heart to shout over the restaurant music to tell him this story about my father. Maybe I felt deep inside it would have been wasted on him.

After the funeral, family members came back to our home for the wake.

One of my dad's sisters said to us, "Your father abandoned us when he went to Australia."

I fled from the lounge room. I am to show respect, regardless of how abominable the things the aunties say are. I covered my face in grief, only to bump into another aunt, this time on my mother's side. My face almost rebounded off her ample chest. I removed my hands from my face as she said, "Why your face like that?" I touched the pimples on my cheeks I had tried to cover with makeup. The tears must have washed it off. I wanted to justify myself, list my reasons: "Because my dad has been dying of cancer. Because I am stressed. Because I am nineteen."

But I did not say anything because, from the time I was a little Asian girl growing up in an Asian house in a Western country, I knew the rules. The rules were to disconnect from myself—my voice, my opinion—and always defer respect to my older relatives. Allow them to be as mean or prying as they liked, as critical and judgmental as they liked, as gossipy and bitchy as they liked and say absolutely nothing. I was worn down by these people. I nodded and excused myself. It was my father's funeral, and it wasn't even safe for me to be me.

It is conflicting because we're programmed to love this family. Some of us develop hard skin, like the outside of a snake fruit, to compensate for this lack of approval and what feels like conditional love paid promptly only on our obedience. Then before we know it, we become adults. We have partners, babies, and the same people who criticized us have done their duty and are bowing out of life. Hunched over in wheelchairs and lying on operating tables, and we are the ones who must care for them. Take them to the toilet, pull up their diapers, and drive them to their doctors' appointments. Our culture tells us to do so. They will never say "thank you" or "sorry." We owe them for the act of birthing us or simply being blood to us. We must reconnect the image of resentment with the image of them diminished, along with a loneliness born of our childhoods' "you're inadequate" theme song, and get on with taking care of them. That's what our filial obligation says, but under this, there is rage. It is a rage of being mute when you want to fight for yourself, and it is a rage not everyone will understand. Many a boyfriend of mine could never understand it because culture is part of my skin; it is there in the almond upturning of my eyes. You can marry into it, you can date it, but it will never be part of you by osmosis.

HUMAN CONNECTION SUPERHERO

My father lived a daily practice of consistently showing up for people. Small kindnesses and acts of service, from cooking delicious meals for Asian students at nearby Murdoch University and hosting them at Easter when they had nowhere else to go, to giving limitless tabs to elderly customers or people who were just scraping by and could not afford their cigarettes and scratch tickets. Whenever I read articles about Teochew people being good at business, I laugh. My sister says, "Dad was the worst at business ever." She's right, but he knew more about human connection than most of us. He knew viscerally because he grew up dirt poor in a house full of addiction and trauma. He knew that possessions, wealth, and achievement do not ever quiet the pain. Connection does. It is the healing balm on the burn trauma leaves behind.

So you can imagine how the trauma of losing my father, in addition to not being soothed as a child, built my "mind-reading" abilities. I had become constantly on edge for tragedy and wildly suspicious of bad news every time I picked up the phone to an unknown number.

So on that summer's day in that Du store in Dubai back in 2013 when my phone rang and my sister's thick Aussie-accented voice—more Julia Gillard than Kylie Minogue—said, "Simone, if I were you, I'd want to come home now," I knew she meant it.

I canceled my flight to my best friend's wedding in Tuscany, which I was set to attend the next day. I booked an eleven-hour direct flight to Perth, and for the whole eleven hours, my heart was pounding in my chest like it would escape my flesh and hurl itself at the seat in front of me. By the time the wheels touched the tarmac at Perth's international airport, that bursting heartbeat had moved down into my stomach until it felt like a wrecking ball breaking me apart.

I went directly in my stale plane clothes to the hospital to see my mother gray and discombobulated in a ward with nauseating cerulean-blue walls. Her legs were spasming, and her eyes were rolling in her head like the small rotating plastic fishing game I had as a child. I had never seen her like this before. She was in a diaper so huge it looked like she was Humpty Dumpty, with her skinny legs out either side. Terrifyingly, she would wear a diaper for the rest of her life. I knew in that moment, as I had when my father died, that my existence would change forever.

FILIAL PIETY

I gripped the railing at the bottom of my mother's hospital bed with white knuckles, looking on in disbelief. One of her eyes rolled again, and she hypnotically yanked her paralyzed left arm, later to be labeled by her caregivers as her "sad arm," over and over again across her body in desperation to see if it could feel something. The universe spoke to me, just whispered in my ear at first, "Simone, you have to come home now."

I dialogued back, "Give up my dream job for someone who was so awful to me growing up?"

When we don't have great self-connection, it's really easy to ignore this internal messaging. This process was the beginning of a cracking open of me, and now, after the healing, I have a self-connection so strong, I can tell you what I am feeling and how I feel about something with a level of visceral storytelling. I didn't have these tools back then.

The other thing about ignoring the universe is that the voice just gets louder. The next day, I went back to see my mother again. I was clean and disinfected and could hold her hand. Again, the whisper came, but this time much louder. It spoke clearly: "Simone, you have to come home now."

I spoke forcefully back to the voice in my head, matching its intensity. "Give up everything I have built for a woman who never gave me the love I needed?" The universe was momentarily silenced. Over the next week, I went to the home I had grown up in between hours at the hospital. Doctors spoke in hushed tones to my sister and me that she would never walk again. I began slowly trying to appraise what my family home had morphed into. My eyes wept from the dog feces stuck to the carpets and the realization of the state that my mother had lived in during those final years. But more on that later.

I went to the bathroom where she had been found. Luckily, that day family friends had been waiting for her to show up for dinner. She had had the final stroke, the stroke that puts all sufferers of that rare disease in a wheelchair, in the shower. The disease takes their legs like Ursula, the sea witch in *The Little Mermaid*, until they are on their back, naked and writhing. That night I showered in that same shower, imagining my mother terrified, trembling at the bottom of it in a pool of her own waste. I imagined how long she lay there horrified, with the scalding hot water she loved to shower in beating down on her face. The water must have been blinding when they busted the door in and had the ambulance take her away.

As the same water traveled down my forehead, the universe howled.

"Simone, you MUST come home NOW!" it screamed so loudly that I gasped, hot water almost choking me. I had no rebuttal. The next day, I visited my mother to say goodbye before returning to Dubai to pack up my life there. My mind already made up that I would repatriate. My mother clutched my hand with her spidery good right fist and drew me close. She spoke in a tone I had never heard from her lips but had wanted to my entire childhood: "Please don't leave me like this. Please come back and take care of me."

She had always taught us that vulnerability was for the weak by her behavior. Here, born of fear, it had the incredible power to connect us. It also holds the key to all truly real human connection. It would go on to become a huge part of my life once I got the hang of it.

"Of course, Mama," I said, tears streaming down my face.

Within six months of packing up my life as an expat in Dubai, I was back in my hometown and totally naive about how useful I would be in my mom's new normal. I thought me just being her daughter and being there would be enough. I wasn't totally off the mark. We now know that stroke victims get more resilience from further complications through having in-person connection than they do from medication, but I wasn't aware of any of this at the time, and the self-loathing and purposelessness soon set in.

You see, my mom is what they call a "two-person assist." This means she consistently requires two people to care for her at all times. To take her from the bed to the toilet, from the toilet to the dining room, and back again. Every time she moves, she needs two caregivers because she cannot walk. I get asked by my Asia-based friends why we don't just get her a helper, which would be normal in the Asian context where labor is bought from the Philippines and Indonesia. Small brown women of incredible patience and fortitude help so that the elderly do not have to be put into homes and can cohabitate with their grandkids in multigenerational households. The backs of caregivers the world over have been broken by trying to take fully grown men from their beds to their wheelchairs. To protect caregivers in Australia, the "two-person assist" rule came into play. It means my mom has to wait a little longer to go to the toilet, but it's more humane on caregivers this way.

In fact, they took and still take such good care of my mother with processes such as this, I was rendered useless. I would sit next to her in the nursing home for five to six hours a day and watch without being able to help. This sense of uselessness and purposelessness was also what contributed to my disconnection from the world. The only thing that saved me was watching my mother's suffering and clinging to the rationality that she was experiencing far worse than me. Her days consisted of diet desserts, reading outdated copies of *Woman's Day*, and trying to keep her eyes open for the weeknight game shows on Channel Nine. She raged against the indignity of not being allowed back into her own home without the assistance of another person and the complete demoralization of having to ring a bell and wait for someone else to come and wipe her butt on the toilet.

FORGIVENESS

One day, after months of watching this happen from her room floor, where I often lay on a spare duvet, I asked her caregivers if I could at least do something. I needed to be of use; that's how I was raised. I had seen so much already, but I was not prepared for this. This was the day, the moment, I finally saw my mother for who she actually was. Not who she had projected into the world but a glimpse into who she may have been before the world embittered her. The Sandra before she was a Heng, before she was a mother, before she was a teacher.

They agreed to let me help take her to the toilet. I opened the door to the bathroom. There she stood, face pressed nose to the white tiled wall, two meters directly in front of me. Her hands were now the ones gripping, white-knuckled, to the metal railing in this bathroom. She was standing, and I realized I hadn't seen her stand for over a year. Wearing a shirt but no pants, her thin legs like toothpicks, muscles atrophied from being wheelchair-ridden. She gripped hard to keep balance, and one caregiver swooped in to prop her up on her weak left side because she was swaying side to side, like a bird with a broken wing. I noticed, with amusement, a printed image of George Clooney on the bathroom wall, almost touching her face. Last week it had been Prince Harry. She had asked the home to print these, so she could have something good to look at during this daily process. But the part that broke my heart, as I glanced down again, was seeing her legs bare, blouse still on, standing there in a diaper. The sheer lack of dignity. My mother had been a tiger, authoritative and powerful. I had never seen her this vulnerable except for the day of my father's funeral. So here was Mom, completely disconnected from her identity. The strong replaced by the "weak."

I had just one job. While the caregiver propped my mother up with one arm, they would then pull her diaper down with their other hand. The other caregiver would push the commode in under her before she lost stability, and all I had to do was pull the wheelchair back and out of the bathroom to give them some space. I had one job to do, but I was horrified. I was frozen seeing this person who had lauded power and criticism over me diminished to this. To a macabre ballet barre routine to undress and do a shit. This woman who had had so much influence over me that, even though I ran from her, put oceans between us, her voice would still ring in my head for every action I took. Her influence was reduced to this. My mother caught my crumbling face of horror in the bathroom mirror. I quickly readjusted and put on my "media face." The eyes frozen and pupils dilated, the mouth tightly pulled upwards by force like a news anchor into a fake smile. After this incident, it would take me six years until I would smile a full sincere smile again, the "Duchenne smile," where my Asian eyes crinkle sincerely in their corners.

"Are you okay, darling?" my mother asked. The "darling" part had become new vernacular since the stroke. She was softening. "I am fine, Mum," I lied, rolling the wheelchair backward into her room. I sat slumped on the edge of her bed that had been pimped out with hydraulics and an air mattress to prevent bedsores. It sighed beneath the weight of me. I sobbed. The deepest sobs. Like an animal, like I heard her cry as she walked in front of my father's hearse. This was inherited pain, transferrable keening. In that moment, I saw a flash of my mother for the sum of all her experiences, and I forgave her for everything. For the fear she lauded over us, the chaotic house, and the lack of emotional support. To understand how monumental this moment was, I have to take you back to where it all began.

CHAPTER 3

TRAUMA

If You Are Loved You Learn to Love

S ingapore was always termed "home" in our family. When I was about eleven, I did a migrant's writing course with my mom, and I wrote a piece where I, too, called Singapore home, not computing that these were simply my parents' words, like an echo I was programmed to repeat. It wasn't "home" to me. I had never lived there except for three years as a baby. I remembered nothing of it. Singapore was painted as a food-filled, fast-paced haven in my parents' nostalgia. Perth, by my reality, was dull in comparison, filled with trips to Sunday church and Saturdays in Chinese class. One day, when I was twelve and feeling brave, I asked my mother, "If Singapore was so wonderful, why did you leave?"

Like most migrant parents, Asian or otherwise, my mother said, "Because we wanted a better life for you children." And then she added, "In Singapore, when we left, all children had to take their father's race's language as their assessed second language at school. You children would have to speak and write Mandarin, and your father only speaks dialects and Malay. I don't speak Mandarin, so you would never make it.

You would have never been able to compete. We wanted you to have a chance to get into university."

This exchange made me feel like I owed my mother the entire act of migration to a place she would rather not be. This is important for what happens in later chapters, but this deep sense of owing our parents is steeped in a Singaporean upbringing. We carry not only the pressure of academic performance but also the pressure of having been given life. It's the stuff of Asian American stand-up comedy but underneath the laughs is the profound understanding that you cannot MESS UP. MESSING UP is not an option, ever. And it's this pressure that started my disconnection because I was no longer connecting to my family as a child or as a human. I was connecting as a vehicle for either success or shame for myself and the whole family. This is where relational loneliness can begin for many, feeling a sense of disconnection and a lack of acceptance within your own home.

I equated this feeling of not completely belonging and not being good enough with unlovability. The way my mother parented was to give me almost enough love as to motivate me to do better. My counselor calls it 80 percent love. The thrilling 100 percent love would be doled out sparingly based on outstanding performance as a tool to affirm. This communicated to me from a very young age that love and affection existed but were being withheld. I eventually made the connection as a child that love for me was conditional and paid only upon suffocating obedience and achievement.

I still have moments now where I have to catch the way I talk to myself and my partner in the same "tough love" tone that my mother spoke to me. There is a part of all of us that is in automation loving others the way we were loved. Our brains are biologically affected by how we were treated and loved as young children. How we make meaning of relationships becomes wired by these early experiences, and it stays with us for the rest of our lives.

In his book with Oprah, *What Happened to You?*, Dr. Bruce D. Perry sums up this idea that our ability to create healthy and genuine human connection in our lives is the direct result of the human connection we received as a child: "The attentive, loving behaviors [of caregivers] grow the neural networks that allow us to feel love, and then act in loving ways towards others. If you are loved, you learn to love."

TOGETHER BUT ALONE

We've all been in a room surrounded by people but still felt lonely. People can physically be there, but that doesn't mean they are connecting with us. Now imagine that those same people are your family. I experienced deep relational loneliness, and a lot of it was tied to culture. Before we dive deeper into my childhood, I want to preface this by saying the antidote to loneliness is love and connection. The quest for my mother's love and our eventual forgiveness has been the true love story of my life. And maybe for many children, Asians in particular, the thirst for approval, validation, and love from our parents follows us for years and years and years. It's not the easiest thing to explain to people who grew up with outwardly approving, expressive, and supportive parents, but criticism and an absence of praise defined my upbringing.

Brené Brown describes the repercussions of not having our needs for love and connection met in childhood in her book *The Gifts of Imperfection*: "When those needs are not met, we don't function as we are meant to. We break. We fall apart. We numb. We ache. We hurt others. We get sick."[13]

The limiting belief that I was unlovable followed me from the day I was born until I was thirty-four years old. It flung me into a perpetual survival mode, and this sabotaged my ability to connect with others.

SENSING WE WERE DIFFERENT

Growing up in Australia, my strict Singaporean parents would not allow us to sleep over at other people's homes. We were lucky to be allowed to go to school camps. As a result of this, I never quite realized that the shouting, the mess, the chaos, and constantly living on the emotional knife's edge of my childhood was different. In my gut, I knew I was much more stressed than my friends at school. I was in a constant state of alert around my mother's moods, but I was too young to make the connection. My childhood was marked with ever-changing states out of my control, and children need a consistent nurturing environment to feel safe and thrive. My mother was dealing with her own demons, born of the rare degenerative disease she has. At the time, there were no studies written about this condition. Many decades later, we now know that symptoms of depression, mood swings, migraines, and blackouts have been exhibited in sufferers as young as eighteen. This has been a large part of the forgiveness that underpins our relationship. Back in 1995, however, we blamed her mood swings, disorganization, and locking herself in her room simply as menopause.

Unpredictability in a primary caregiver, even from infancy, deeply affects how a child creates their worldview. I long held a narrative that people were unpredictable and not to be wholly trusted based not only on my mother's mood swings but also the turbulent relationships and gossip that characterized some of my extended family's relationships. Living with this distress put me out of balance, and feeling I was unlovable deeply affected how I connected with other people.

My mother and father were married at twenty-one and twenty-four and then tried to conceive babies for thirteen years. As a result of the decade-and-a-half wait, I was born when my mother was in her late thirties. Normal for the era we live in now, but very late compared to her peers. I always felt my parents couldn't keep up because they were older than my friends' parents by over a decade. The house was so disorganized, and the sheer chaos of being in that house felt terrifying to me as a child. There was no routine. Lights were broken and not fixed for years. No fresh fruit or vegetables in the fridge. My mother was the biggest fan of canned food; I didn't even know it was not good for children until a friend at school told me. Toast and canned soup was her favorite thing to feed us on weekends. I would often eat cake for breakfast if an aunty had dropped some off, which was the only nonexpired food in the fridge.

Our clothes were washed on an ad-hoc basis. Once I got old enough, I learned to use the hand wash basin when I'd run out of fresh underwear because I was scared of putting the wrong items in the washing machine and breaking something that would cause me to be shouted at for days. The disorganization and lack of clocks that worked in those analog days meant my parents could never manage time. There was always shouting before needing to leave for any outings. We had pets that my mom treated terribly, as if the dogs were there to be cheap guards for her house versus being pets to be cared for. I remember when I went back home for a trip when I was living in Dubai and found her Doberman in the backyard with rashes and flies gnawing off the flesh around his anus. She hadn't washed him for years. I wanted to hold him, but he was skittish from neglect. I looked into his sad eyes and recognized my own as a child.

Yet when it came to saving face, my parents were fantastic.

My mom would make us clean the house all day if we were having people over. She would bring out the best table settings. My father would go to Fremantle Markets and buy the most succulent squid and prawns. "Four times the size of those in Singapore!" he would proclaim, still impressed after a decade in Australia. I would relish these gatherings because I would know we would enjoy reduced shouting from my mom in front of other people and have leftover real, tasty food in the fridge for a few days. I vowed when I grew up that I would never live like this.

In addition to being a generation apart from my peers' parents, mine were also a culture apart. By the time I was a teenager, my mother was going through menopause. She'd had a full hysterectomy. I remember her being mad at us all the time. I felt I was a total inconvenience. Her behavior was incongruous to me because it didn't match my father's stories about how long they tried for babies. Finally, they found a doctor to treat her endometriosis, and my sister was born; I was an added bonus two years later.

One evening when I was nine, the *Grease* movies were back-to-back on TV in one of their marathon promotions. One of the lead actors, Jeff Conway, played the villain Kenickie and had the same deep acne scars along his face as my mom. My observation as a child was as innocent as running your hand through sand at the beach and noticing texture. I just connected those same scars on Kenickie's face to the ones I saw on her. I ran to her as she was seated on the couch. She never hugged us; I longed to be held by my mother. I raised my hand to try and touch her cheek, and she grabbed my hand before I could. I said to her, "Mommy, you have the same skin as Kenickie. What is this?"

She pushed me off her and got off the couch. She was enraged. I was petrified when she would get like this. I felt stupid and awash with shame that I had even tried to touch her. She retorted, "Yes, you children destroyed my face."

I had no idea what this meant and was too scared to ask. Many years later, I finally asked my father, and he replied, "Your mom had to take some very crude hormone medication to conceive, and that's how her skin became like that."

I felt I owed my mother her skin, her beauty, her migration. I carried this burden with me for my entire childhood like a sack of bricks on my back, and it cornered me into my decision to leave Dubai and be with her in 2014.

TOP MARKS IN THE CLASS

As I grew older, the dysfunction with which I learned to relate to my mother was hardwired into me. I had a deep fear of her and had developed a trauma-altered stress response. Things that my peers at school found trivial weighed heavy on me with pressure. I remember losing three marks on an English paper in high school. Twenty-two out of twenty-five. I was proud of it; it was the top grade in the class. After school, I announced it buoyantly to my mom, sweat still in the small of my back from walking my huge textbooks home in the thirty-five-degree heat.

"I was top of the class for this paper, Mom," I announced, waving it in sweaty palms.

The words "top of the class" were like an addictive *Daily Mail* headline to my mom. The kind of statement that would stimulate a jolt from her on the couch, particularly if someone else's child was "top of something." My voice was trembling, trying to conceal the straining for her approval. My heart was palpitating, yearning that she would be in a good mood today to hear this news. Yearning, as always, that she would see me fully.

My mother looked at the score scrawled in red pen with

a circle around it at the top of the page and, without smiling, shook her head. "That score makes top of the class." She almost spit the words with disgust.

She tutted, in the same way most of the Asian migrant mothers would, at the complete indulgence of the Australian school system. As if they were owed better for the trouble of migrating. That the system was building slovenly, lazy children. As if they didn't already know they had come to a place where everyone, and I mean everyone, who wants in gets into university. Isn't that why they chose Australia?

This was followed by, "Go back into class and ask Mrs. M where you lost the three marks."

Her tone let me know she meant it.

I was mortified. What could be less cool and more foreign to my Australian teacher than having to do this? In years to come, I would understand that what my mother was actually giving me was a profound gift. She was teaching me to fight for myself in the world. To not take less than the best to avoid the mediocrity from setting into my bones like wood rot. Being average, I was led to believe, was contagious. But on the other hand, always needing to fight for yourself makes life a fight, and it is exhausting. I see that now in my mother's sunken cheeks and paralyzed face, the face of a person for whom life was a grasping fight to control. Life finally taught her that it would not be tamed when it took my father. Life betrayed her by incentivizing her daughter to always live far away. I look at her with love, but I am glad I unplugged and deprogrammed.

CONFRONTING AUTHORITY

It was a balmy three o'clock in the afternoon. Friday Perth sun streaming into the classroom, threatening to expose my hot cheeks and shame. I could hear the sounds of other kids giggling, chatting excitedly about their weekend. That's how I saw a lot of my childhood: me being forced to do something inside while other kids, white kids, were outside having what seemed to be deep bottomless blue swimming pools of fun.

On school holidays, I would stand helping my dad serve customers at his shop and tiptoe enough to crane my neck over the kiosk counter and see other kids riding the mall's mechanical animal ride and licking ice cream drips off chubby, sweaty hands. Laughing. I was envious. Deep emerald crystallized envy. And yet, working and being diligent when others weren't became part of me. Even as I write this, it is Sunday morning in Singapore, and while I can hear my partner outside laughing with my puppy, I am still inside working. It is not strange to me. It is part of me, like the warm remnant of heat off a parent's hug I rarely felt. I work because it reminds me of them; it's all I have left of them.

My hands trembled with rage as I pushed forward the paper to Mrs. M, the paper once pushed with decisive pride to my mother, now quivering from those same hands like sails on a boat within a furious sea. I felt enraged at myself that my mother was putting me up to this and even more enraged that I was so programmed to obey. I knew that night when she came home dog-tired from work, too tired even to cook or buy us food to eat, that she would NEVER forget to ask about my education. EVER. I opened my mouth to speak and said, "Mrs. M, my mom wants me to ask where I have missed out on these three marks and why."

Mrs. M, a kind, patient woman, had children of her own in our school. She was a mother. In my maladapted narrative of people, which I explained earlier, I felt sure she was just sick of Asian parents and Asian migrant kids keeping her behind after work because of their own cultural hang-ups. Haggling for grades must have seemed distant and foreign to her, not to mention undermining her authority. As she spoke, like many moments you'll hear about in this book, my mind left my body. Her lips moved, but I heard nothing but the shame of it all, my being deprived of fun, the chaos and shouting of insults in my house, the lack of nonexpired food in the fridge when I wanted something to eat while studying for grades that my existence depended on, the fear of my mother's mood swings—all of it made tears roll down my face. I felt tired. I was fourteen, but yet I felt tired.

"Yes, and now I see we have the tears again," said Mrs. M.

My brain returned to my body. I snapped back into reality. I will never forget that line for as long as I live. That I must have had conversations with her before where I broke under the pressure of what was expected of me. To me, the skepticism on her tongue meant she couldn't possibly understand me, and it just affirmed the lack of trust in people that I had already been forming. She couldn't imagine what it was like to live in my house. My house with its lack of psychological safety. A house so large but so empty of the things kids need. *Mrs. M has no idea,* I thought. *She has kids, she deals with hundreds of kids, and she thinks this is a put-on melodrama? She thinks my family is what my mother makes us project. Churchgoing, award-winning, respectful, don't-ask-for-anything immigrants, and how dare I now ask for this!* I vowed never to show vulnerability again, and I didn't for twenty-two years. In its place, I put ambition because ambition would put oceans between me and this place where no one understood me.

FIRST LOVE

In Dubai at twenty-four, I fell head over heels for the kindest man I have ever met. He loved me with a ferocity I have since never known, a ferocity we feel when we fall for the first time. Things were great until I found myself picking fights and pointing out flaws. I could not let us slip into calm. It had to be the roller coaster of feelings; it had to be a tugging and wrestling for even more love as if I needed 120 percent to make up for the 80 percent I experienced my whole childhood. It almost broke him. Now he was the exhausted one. I had to be in fight-or-flight for anything to be real, to feel anything. This is the stamp of trauma on our psyche, like a cattle brand on your heart. This is how it sabotages your human connections. You will relive the conditions of your childhood home in your relationships with other people, in the workplaces you choose and the friendships you stay in, until you see the pattern clearly and seek help.

There was mercy in that relationship ending; I would have destroyed him over time. He deserved and got better from someone else, and I dragged my feet into therapy a decade later to ask tepidly, "Is love always meant to feel like this?" The answer was "No," and that's how my journey to healing began.

JUXTAPOSITION

Remember I mentioned I had to move four thousand kilometers away to confirm that the way I grew up was different from that of my peers? I had passed off most crazy things as "just being an immigrant kid" rather than acknowledging my hunch that the chronic stress was damaging me. At age eighteen, I secured an exchange to study in Switzerland. Over the course of a year, I lived with three different families. Each family was delightful in their own way. My first family was mixed Swiss-Argentinian, and they are literally the most generous people I have ever met in my entire life. The children in this family loved each other deeply and truly treated me as if I was their own sibling. There was never fighting, shouting, or raised voices. Both my host parents worked, and the house was still spotless. My mother had always said our house was messy because she had to work so hard, but here was evidence that everyone could work *and* wash clothes *and* buy food for their children. We also had a cleaning lady once a week growing up, and there were still no fresh groceries on the regular. The penny started dropping.

My second host family barely spoke any English. Their kids had long grown up and, in their retirement, they were kind enough to house an exchange student. This was the first time in my life that a mother made me a packed lunch with so much care that I wanted to cry. Vreni would make me Swiss Bircher muesli and separate the grated apple for me so that when I went to school, I could mix it in, and it would still be nice and crunchy. I had never seen mothering like this. Mom, at the height of her moods, would give us a can of Campbell's soup to take to school still condensed and ask me to tell the lunch lady to open it, warm it up, and mix it in water. Some lunchtimes, by the time I got to the front of the line on a cold winter's day, the bell would ring, and I wouldn't have time to eat, let alone get the can open. My dad would later start allowing me to take coins from his coin bowl so I could buy some proper food to last me through the day.

The last host family I am actually so close with that I consider my host mother to be an actual second mother to me. If COVID-19 hadn't hit, I would be there with her now, writing this book in her winter garden. She was like my real mother in her bold opinions and sassy humor but also deeply domestic. As in the tradition of many Swiss hausfraus, Irene can cook them under the table. In all three of these homes, the energy was calm, the voices low, and the words supportive. It was this emotional experience, living full-time with three very different families in one year, all of whom were consistently loving, that started me suspecting that maybe I wasn't so loathsome, not good enough, and unlovable. Maybe something bigger was at play.

It was also always amazing to me when I moved back to Singapore to work and spoke about these experiences on social media that I would receive message after message that this is how many Singaporean adults my age still feel about their upbringing. There is immense pain carried by a child when they swap their humanness for being a vehicle of shame or success for their family and are constantly criticized for every attempt to bring them pride. This is the root of relational loneliness for us. This whole feeling that made me feel so bad about myself as a child was experienced by not just me, an Asian kid in Australia, but by Asian kids in Asia. And from the hundreds of conversations I have had on it, I think the relational loneliness we experience comes down to one thing: a lack of expression of pride. Now don't get me wrong, I am a proud Asian woman, but I am also an advocate for healthy human connection. So, if a child constantly hears that they are not good enough, that they are underperforming, or, most crushingly, that they are compared to others, that they should be more like their siblings, cousins, or some kid at school with high scores, that is traumatizing to the fragile sense of self they are developing. If in addition to this, they don't get any positive affirmation, it can lead to a lifetime of chasing for validation. And chasing for love, approval, and validation deeply inhibits the formation of healthy adult relationships.[14]

In addition to this, you cannot become great at connecting with others when you don't have a great connection with yourself. It was not until I had the vernacular to say my childhood was traumatic, it was not until the dust of where I came from settled, it was not until I healed after arduous hours in therapy and study that I was truly able to be a decent human connector. To be compassionate and present, to forgive and serve others, this is when my cup runneth over, when the fog of trauma lifted. I of course still fail at it at times, but I am always improving. Looking my childhood in the face, calling out the truth of what it was, I was then able to forgive my mother comprehensively and be at peace with my childhood.

Here are some self-connection challenges that will help you connect better with yourself, others, and your childhood.

CONNECT WITH YOUR CHILDHOOD MEMORIES.

Self-connection is the key to connecting with others. A great place to start the process of knowing ourselves better can be knowing where we came from. Think back to your childhood. Are there any tenuous existing relationships that may need reconnecting? Was there trauma not spoken about or swept under the rug that you have been avoiding sitting with and processing?

REACH OUT FOR HEALING.

Reach out to a sibling or parent and ask them about things that may have been haunting you. Remember that there are multiple truths to any viewpoint. For example, the accounts of Australia being colonized by the British will be very different depending on whether you speak to an Indigenous Australian or a colonizer. Both of these contradicting accounts exist in history. Using this as a metaphor, even if a sibling, parent, or relative doesn't feel the same way about your recollection of an event, it doesn't mean your feelings and version of the event aren't valid.

CONNECT WITH A GREAT COUNSELOR.

If you are aware there is some trauma already, like loss in your direct family, connect with a great counselor or therapist in your area. If you are lost on this, feel free to message me on social media, and I will send you the email of someone who can help.

CHAPTER 4

ADDICTED TO LOVE

The Relationship Between Human Connection
and Addiction

In 2014, after I returned to Perth to help with my mom's transition to the nursing home, she got an infection. I had been called by the nursing home staff and rushed into her room only to see her face red and swollen. At the foot of her bed towered a woman, whom I will call Rhonda. Rhonda had Alzheimer's; she has since passed. She was convinced my mother was her late husband. As I walked in, Rhonda had just slipped out of lucidity and become aggressive.

My mom, unpredictable and sassy, didn't seem frightened at all. Rhonda was almost six feet tall and fully mobile. *If she's this tall now, how tall was she before she started shrinking?* I thought to myself. Nursing homes are full of people shrinking. My mother is tiny and stuck in a bed. Next to Rhonda she looked like a frail lone quail's egg cocooned in a nest of blankets. Fragile. Rhonda gripped the end of the bed and decisively turned her head to me, sneering at my presence, nostrils flared, like a scene from *Jurassic Park* when a T. rex smells a human.

"Who are you?" she snarled.

"I'm Simone, Sandra's daughter. Why are you in my mom's room?" I secretly pressed the call button behind my leg. Here's the thing about dementia: in that moment, Rhonda was, in her mind, possibly her thirty-five-year-old self. She had an energy and posture that went back in time, and her forcefulness could have been that not of a seventy-year-old but someone my age. I could have been flung across the room. One of the things I love the most about my mom's nursing home is that residents who physically can walk are free to do so; you just run the risk of them sometimes walking unannounced into the wrong room that they think is rightfully theirs. This day, it was even more tenuous because Rhonda also thought my mom was her long-dead husband.

"You're not her daughter. That's my husband," she said red-faced.

"Look, Rhonda, Mom's sick. I need to take care of her." My mom looked on amused.

"She's not your mother. What are the names of our children?" she asked us.

"Gerald, Sally, and Andrew," my mother replied, satisfied. She'd tapped into something that I was ignorant of at the time. Firstly, my mother had learned that the best way to handle people with dementia was not to challenge their belief when they were agitated but to go with it. I wondered for a moment where she had learned this nuance. Rhonda was her closest friend and neighbor in the room next door. Mom had already had two new neighbors since then. I thought to myself, *This is how people learn the ropes in prison quickly to survive*. I was proud of my mom that even with her ill, broken brain, she could still adapt and learn. The irony of this now is that her own mind has deteriorated, so we placate her the same way she did Rhonda. We pretend my dad is still alive, that he's just gone on holiday instead of gone into the ground.

At this point, Rhonda started coming at me with her hand raised, and, just at the moment of impact, one of Mom's incredible caregivers swooped into the room. Rhonda paused. Discombobulated. The caregiver grabbed her arm and moved her gently to the next room. Rhonda crumbled, her posture changed. She was lucid again, remorseful, and apologetic for not remembering what she'd done. She folded her six-foot frame what felt like almost half of her height. She was led by the arm to the door, her forearm skin patched like mortadella from years baking under the Australian sun. She was guided by the plump brown hand of her caregiver. Skin made in Manila, brown skin that sought a better life in Australia only to wipe the butts of the elderly daily for a tiny wage and never to complain. Make it look easy. Do it with grace. Take abuse. They are walking saints.

Mom's caregiver returned to tell me, "Your mother has an infection for sure. Her fever is very high, but it's a Friday evening, and the doctor can't come until Monday. So, you can wait until then or call an ambulance and take your mom to the emergency at the hospital now to see a doctor."

The same hospital where it all began a year or so earlier when I had walked in, fresh from that plane from Dubai, to see my mom gray-skinned and terrified. She looked rather terrified again in that moment. I asked her if she wanted to go to emergency and noticed the deep rings around her watery green eyes. Her face was totally swollen red in contrast.

I am still trying to wrack my brain now for how I got to the hospital. If I rode in the back with her or took my car or called a cab and followed along. The fact that I cannot remember is a sign of the deep survival mode I must have been in. What I do remember is that I had good cause to be in fight-or-flight because what found us in that hospital on a Friday evening was worth fretting over, and it wasn't actually my mother that I needed to worry about.

SCRATCHING ON PLEXIGLASS

The waiting room, filled with screaming kids with minor injuries like skateboarding accidents, cleared by 10 p.m. The screams or howls were now from adults. Clerks behind plexiglass sheets to protect them. Addicts. Parched skin the texture of a chewed cigarette, eyes hollow and wiry fingers scratching. So much scratching. On skin and clothes, plastic waiting room chairs. I clutched Mom's hand tight at that moment, realizing why she had been so strict my entire childhood. She was protecting us from a subculture our interlocked ethnic conservative Catholic community rarely had seen. I was thirty but still so naive. Then the scratching on the plexiglass turned to a banging. A pregnant woman howled. Her partner, who was wearing a crushed leather jacket and worn cap, brought her forward and begged; they begged for something. They were refused. He became angry. She howled again. I closed my eyes, and for the first time, I felt real fear not from within my own family but from an external threat. I also felt deep fear because this was just another moment where I realized my mother and I had swapped roles. She had been shrunk into my daughter, and I had become her mother. I was mother to a sixty-eight-year-old in diapers.

We were admitted and put into a small, dark room. There was what looked like a white shower curtain creating a barrier to people seeing us outside. The curtain came only halfway up, so I could see the shadows dancing every time someone walked past. My mother was sliding out of her wheelchair now. It was five hours past her bedtime. I put the brakes on her chair, squatted at the knees, and in a chest-touching embrace, dragged her back into the chair. I thought about how many years I wished for that hug as a child and the macabre way in which I got what I wished for so ardently. I held her hand as she slept, my chin resting on the top of the plastic chair and the back of the chair between my legs. This looked like a far more comfortable position in music videos than in reality. I remember the plastic cutting into my thighs as I winced to the sound of the screams.

Friday evening in emergency in that hospital was full of people suffering. Not in the gentle way people slip away in nursing homes like candle wax silently melting but in a violent, excruciating tug-of-war. I wondered how Mom could sleep through it but thought that maybe the nurses had given her sleep meds before we left. I could hear the rustling of a scuffle in the cubicle next door. The in-between-dream-and-awake stage yielding phrases like, "It's okay, you'll be okay" from the medical staff. Intoxicated, indecipherable, slurred speech replying. The whole energy was dark and unyielding, and the way my mother was cared for there was very different from the tenderness given when she had been upstairs in the stroke unit the year before.

I look back and see the young Asian doctor, Malaysian or Singaporean, frantically checking my mom's vitals. Peeling back her diaper quickly to check for a urinary tract infection, rustling it open with haste, the way kids open Happy Meal boxes from McDonald's. Impatient fingers frantic because it was obvious there were bigger things going on that evening in emergency.

Finally, as the sun came up, we were released. I was relieved when it was over; we'd made it through the night. I often wondered what the point was. We essentially had just had our own horrific slumber party. She was made to sleep in a chair, and so was I. She was given some meds, but really there wasn't much change. Then I also realized this was our first overnight evening together since I was a kid. Is that what my mom wanted all along?

A LACK OF CONNECTION LEADS TO ADDICTION

What never left me were the sounds of the screams and my horrific ignorance. My borderline judgment of those suffering because their affliction—addiction—is so much closer to me and to all of us than we would like to think. Addiction expert Dr. Gabor Mate believes that we are all not as distant from addicts as we perceive. That there are so many "behavior addictions" fostered in our current culture, from workaholism to social media addiction, that we can learn a lot from the treatment of addicts on how to heal our own behaviors. Most important to the work in this book, he believes that at the root of the problem is a disconnection. This could be abuse, trauma, or just a "hurt."[15]

In their book *What Happened to You?*, both Dr. Bruce D. Perry and Oprah elaborate on this idea. They state that a lack of human connection as early as infancy, when a child cries for food or to have their diaper changed and their primary caregiver does not respond, can cause the infant to become out of balance and develop chronic distress. They form the worldview that people are not safe or supportive because their basic needs were not met. Ideally, an infant's needs should be soothed in a loving, attentive, consistent environment. This then helps the child associate human connection with reward.

Childhood trauma links so powerfully to human connection and addiction because the child that isn't soothed of their distress goes into chronic fight-or-flight; they become particularly vulnerable to addiction. The addictive substances or behaviors are used to regulate their trauma-altered stress response and provide respite from this chronic distress. This is what makes addictions so hard to shake because the relief is sometimes the first time an individual has felt calm and balanced in their entire existence, and that yearning for peace and calm keeps pulling them back in. Individuals who have their needs for human connection met in early childhood can more easily resist being pulled back into an addictive behavior because that chronic distress is not there, constantly pleading to be calmed.

LOVE, ADDICTION, AND THE SEARCH FOR CONNECTION

Many years after my fearful experience with my mother in the basement of that hospital, I learned in therapy that a large part of the source of my personal hurt and pain stemmed simply from feeling unlovable. I was a love addict, someone in constant search for connection, with a deep thirst for love and approval. In each new person I met, I didn't see a human, I saw a vessel for possible validation and adoration, which I equated with being loved for a fleeting moment. This is why so many personalities like mine choose occupations in the public eye, to soothe the pain of unlovability through the love they perceive fame as. Yet fame is the opposite of connection. Even at my low levels of notoriety, I have found that fame is people connecting with an avatar of you that you construct versus who you actually are.

It's hard for me to write. Human connection was something I deeply craved, but as I mentioned earlier, the act of chasing after it repelled it further. Learning to connect with myself and then connecting better with others healed me. Of course, there are many moments I still get triggered, but I have stopped irrationally trying to chase love and authentic connection from everyone. I am at peace with the fact that not everyone is for everyone. Finding genuine human connection, deep love, and acceptance among my intimate relationships, family and friends, and a group with a collective purpose was the direct route to my healing. Obliterating all three orbits of loneliness was the answer. It has taken and still takes a lot of work to align those three orbits of connection, but it's my hope that through this book's connection challenges, I will be able to provoke you into starting on that same journey.

HOW CONNECTION HEALS

So how do we heal? On a video conference with me, Helen, a thirty-seven-year-old Singaporean woman who calls herself an "alcoholic in recovery," says she reminds herself to remain devoted to the process of healing, that she isn't fixed and perfect yet. She's been in active recovery for eight years and began drinking at age eight. From her first sip, she always wanted more: "It's a physical dependency and also a mental obsession, so it's a mind-and-body thing that affects me. Alcohol was my mother, my father, my lover, my everything up until the point it failed me."

Prior to the second year of sobriety, Helen says she "acted like an orphan," like she didn't have a family and recently made amends with her mother to whom she was estranged for sixteen years.

Human connection has been a key tool in her healing, functioning in three ways. Firstly, through self-connection. The moment she realized alcohol no longer served to give her the effect she wanted, that her body could literally no longer keep it down, was the moment she knew she had to let it go. Secondly, recovery groups ended her collective loneliness by connecting her to a tribe with a common understanding: "I had never identified a group of people or friends before. My best friend helped me understand what the twelve-step recovery group did for me when she said, 'Helen, thank God you finally found a group of people who understand you in a way that we never could.' I identified like-minded people in meetings who shared the same affliction. People who were laughing through darkness and understood that darkness. I felt connection."

Lastly, part of her recovery was completely relearning to connect with others again, getting to know her true self completely apart from her addictive behaviors. From here, she began to make amends in her relationships that she lost through her addiction: "I had to learn to crawl again. Open a letter without drinking. How to answer the phone without drinking. How to connect to someone outside of a recovery room. How to even connect with my own husband while not drinking. I had to work to be the best version of myself, to be the best version for them. A better wife, a better friend, a better daughter, a better sister. The closer I am connected to something bigger than me—that includes being of service, support, and helping others—the further away I am from a drink."

So if, like me, you've felt the burn of unlovability and you suspect your needs for support, love, and connection weren't met in childhood, it's absolutely not too late to heal addictive behaviors. It starts by building strong orbits of people around you who authentically care for you, spend time with you, and support you. This is the first step to moving from unhealthy soothing of your distress.

In the words of Dr. Bruce D. Perry: "Connectedness counters the pull of addictive behaviors. It is the key."[16]

Addict or not, here's what we can learn from the relationship between human connection and addiction.

SHARE YOUR PAIN.

Self-connection, that process of "connecting with the worthiness and wholeness of your Self," as Tim Sitt defines it, is key. I was unaware for decades that I had a love addiction, and it was deeply affecting how I connected with others. When painful feelings arise, are there parts of your life you gloss over, choosing to push down and not process, favoring other behaviors? If so, how can you slowly lean into remembering, processing, and maybe eventually sharing those moments with a trusted intimate connection?

THINK ABOUT YOUR FAMILY HISTORY.

Healthy family relationships are vital. This is where we first learn about human connection. Were there feelings of not belonging and unlovability? Were your needs met for attention, support, and basic resources? I know it is daunting, but how can you reach out and make amends for your part in the disconnection of those relationships?

SERVE OTHERS.

As Helen mentioned, her life got better when she could be of service and support to others. This is one of the most beneficial elements of addiction support groups. Are there people who are at risk, or are there addicts in your family or close circle? How could you support them in their recovery?

CHAPTER 5

ATROPHY

The Effect of Isolation on How We Connect

I want you to imagine it's 2025, five years from our global lockdown due to COVID-19, and we now don't have to commute to work every single day. You just go in two to four days a week and only really for in-person communication and meetings. While working in virtual teams during the pandemic, we all realized that people were more energized and seemed to pay much more attention if a meeting was in-person versus a video conference. Human connection, we realized, also helps engagement and productivity.

Prior to COVID-19, you may have worked in a shiny office tower in a multistory building with different workplaces. Often when you'd go to work, you would bump into people getting coffee who weren't from your workplace, you'd talk about your children or the project you're working on, or how stressed you may be feeling. You wouldn't just laugh and share mutual experiences; you'd also learn about how somebody else did business. You'd often think in these moments how these microconnections, small incidental conversations, made you feel better. They were also valuable in sparking creativity and problem-solving.

But that all seems like ancient history now. Since COVID-19 and the recession that followed, many businesses have downsized, and now your workplace is in a purpose-built facility. Inside this building are only the people you work with, people you already know. Your life has literally become the connections within your household, your family, your existing friends, and your existing colleagues. There are very few brand-new interactions you're experiencing day-to-day in person.[17]

Despite high vaccination rates, new flu viruses are a possibility and parts of the population choosing to remain unvaccinated also pose a risk. In an effort to minimize any future re-lockdowns, your workdays alternate with other people on your team so there won't be the full workforce commuting at peak hour together or in the office at the same time. On this day, you walk into the brand-new building for the first time since its completion. It makes a nice change to working at home. You exhale a sigh of relief, grateful that you're not in a mask. You look around and notice that the new hallways have been made extra wide, so there's never a possibility to brush shoulders with anyone.

You walk up to the sleek, touchless elevator and admire the sensors. You enter the office. You can still see everyone, but they've placed plexiglass sheets inside the office floor, so if there's a new outbreak, a button can be pressed, and these sheets can be raised, creating safer cubicles. You can see the workmen testing the sheets now; they're propelling upwards like toast popping. It's smart, you think, then work can continue as normal with less fear of contamination. You can still see your team, but you certainly can't touch. You make a mental note to buy some plants to make your workspace look less like a hospital.

You put your bag down at your seat, look at your watch, and realize all this touring means you're late. It's already time for your one in-person meeting of the day. Although you no longer have to wear masks, you still have to sit a meter away from the rest of your colleagues. When the meeting is over, you go back to your desk, and as you're tapping away at your laptop, you think to yourself, "Everything that I can do here today, I can do from my house." So, you jump back on the train to go home. You and your partner have moved farther out from the city because, as you don't have to commute as much, there wasn't much of a point paying high rent, and now at least the kids have more time to run about in the bigger house. You look around the train carriage and notice how few people there are. You nod and try to smile at a couple of people, but they are all looking down at their phones. Wistfully, you then bow your head as well and look at yours.

Once you get to your house and race up to your home office for your next call, you close your eyes and relish the silence of your space, which you soundproofed when the whole COVID-19 situation started dragging into years. You can no longer hear the sounds of the postman dropping the mail off or the footsteps of your neighbors' kids when they run home from school, or even the sound of the dogs barking. You have effectively blocked out the sound of your tribe. The human tribe.

THE SCIENCE BEHIND LESS TOUCH

So how will our lives be affected by a future with less touch? Where the corridors to our buildings are built wider, where the fear of a new virus encourages us to stay a meter apart. I interviewed James Coan, the director of the Virginia Affective Neuroscience Laboratory at the University of Virginia. He says that touch is so powerful because it communicates to our brains that we have more resources beyond ourselves, reminding us of the human tribe we are part of and the safety that comes with being in numbers:

> The first thing that not having touch is going to do to you is make you more anxious because one of the purposes of touch is to tell your brain that it has less work to do when it comes to being vigilant for potential threats. It's not just any touch but if it's your partner who's touching you and you have a trusting, high-quality relationship, then your brain is going, "Okay, it's not just my two eyes here that are watching the world. It's also my partners'."[18]

We need touch to make us feel safer. So, in a world where we are deprived of touch, we will experience less calm. It isn't normal to us. A lack of touch makes us less calm.

THE COSTS OF LONELINESS

What are some of the other costs besides missing human touch? The costs of what I have termed the "secret pandemic." Anxiety and depression are certainly part of it. We are going to see a global mental health crisis over the next few years as the ripples of the effects of social distancing reach outwards. As I mentioned earlier in this book, I lost one of my dearest friends to suicide during the height of the first wave and similar losses have been seen over and over again since COVID-19 began.

This could be because loneliness creates a cycle, leading to more isolation. Here's how Dr. Coan explains what's happening in our lonely brains:

> What happens when you're lonely is that you become starved. It's like being malnourished. You are constantly running in a kind of deficit with that bioenergetic resource. And so, your brain starts looking for ways to not spend any energy. So, you sleep all day, you avoid anything that seems like it might cause you another stress response, and that avoidance becomes a cycle and you become isolated.
>
> When we're lonely, the stakes become higher and what we do is we paradoxically hold people to higher standards, even though we need people desperately. We require more evidence that they're really going to be there for us. And that keeps us trapped in a cycle of loneliness because we hold people very often to a higher standard than is reasonable.

The second cost of social isolation is social awkwardness. What Dr. Coan describes is really the beginnings of the outbursts and misreading of social cues; the social awkwardness then repels connection. It is something I have experienced viscerally following my mother's illness. Your social skills, like muscles in your body, atrophy when not being used. A *New York Times* article with the teaser "We're All Socially Awkward Now" described these symptoms as oversharing on office video calls because you're so thirsty for connection, wanting so badly to be around people. Once around them, however, you want to retreat, you feel overwhelmed, and this overwhelming sensation often also leads to a misreading of social cues. This is how the loneliness cycle showed up in my life.

SCREAMING FOR CONNECTION WITH THINGS

When I repatriated to be with Mom after the stroke, as the second punch in the face that happens when people we love become incapacitated, I had to take care of all of the stuff that she accumulated in her life and left behind.

And for me, because my father passed away too, that was seventy years of their belongings, thirty-five years of each of their stuff. My mother was a hoarder—is a hoarder, I should say. And before you laugh at that, hoarding is to me, someone who experienced it at ground zero, one of the worst symptoms of loneliness there is. This is because it starts with loneliness and then leads to more loneliness, simply as the result of how the collection of stuff physically isolates the hoarder. Hoarding, I have learned, is screaming out because you're lonely but with possessions. It isn't an inkling red flag in your stomach anymore, it's a SCREAMING for connection. It was only in 2013 that hoarding was included in the *Diagnostic and Statistical Manual of Mental Disorders (DSM-5)*. But while they were busy classifying it, I was buried nose-deep, cleaning it. We knew so little about it. The vast majority of people with hoarding disorder (92 percent) also have another psychiatric disorder. Dementia and organic brain syndromes are very common among people with hoarding disorder (HD). So yes, it's an actual mental disorder like depression, but it still isn't seen that way in the eyes of most people. It's still shrouded in shame and ridicule.[19] My hope is that what you read next in this chapter will help to destigmatize it.

SCULPTURES OF LOSS

In 2014, after Mom became ill and her memory became more patchy, I began asking aunts and uncles to help me learn more about who my parents were before they had children.

One aunt had said my mother was extremely house proud, wrapping bricks with the same fabric as the curtains to create some sort of DIY matching doorstops. Hey, it was the '80s. Despite my personal aversion to matchy-matchiness, this story sounded like a mother I knew up until the age of ten. A mother who would book us into plaster painting and flower arrangement classes on school holidays. Hoarding, I then realized, is a coping mechanism of hers to the trauma of losing so much. It wasn't her personality.

The cleanup of your parents' things is not something you can outsource. You can uncover some horrible secrets that no one else outside of your family should see. You will lose face. I have a friend who found presents that her father wrapped for his mistress. I have another who found letters her mother had written to the Vatican begging for a divorce from her father. My disconnection from the world started because, unlike when my father died or people pass away, the community gets it, and they rally around you to help. But with hoarding disorder, people don't understand it. It's not something about which I can say, "Hey, can you please come and help support me cleaning my mother's thirty-five-year accumulation of trash?" The hoarding atrophied my social skills because I quit my job again, this time on the radio in Australia. And from 9:00 a.m.–5:00 p.m. every day for six months, I cleaned. I stopped seeing people, I stopped reaching out to people. Sorting the hoard became my life. I lay every night exhausted by the process of sifting through stuff and dreading getting up the next day with barely any sleep to start cleaning again. Through the cleaning, I could literally track my mother's disconnection with the world through possessions. What I learned is etched on my memory forever. Where I once saw a pile of clothes, I now see sculptures of loss. Tributes to trauma.

I found enough rubber bands to melt into a basketball, quilting magazine after quilting magazine after quilting magazine. And then the feces of those Maltese terriers stuck to the carpet, turning white, that my mother had piled more things over. Large yellow dog pee stains on antique Chinese carpets she had migrated to Australia with, so precious to her that as children, we were not even allowed to have drinks in our hands when stepping over them. To allow things to become like this, I knew there must have been a cracking of the mind, a letting go completely of any standard that connected her to social norms.

We had a nine-bedroom family home as an antidote to small-apartment living in Singapore. My parents had built this huge, 1980s colossus with glass blocks like something out of *Scarface*. The house had high ceilings and was painted completely in white. Even a simple child's birthday party would leave horrifying powdered chocolate fingerprints from birthday cakes on every banister. I would proudly, and without thinking it a slight, call it "the messy mansion" to my visiting Singaporean relatives who "oohed" and "ahhed" at its basketball hoop in the driveway and swimming pool in the backyard. It was almost always messy, yet we were made to clean furiously for those visits, keeping up the facade that the shopkeeper in Australia could have the house of the millionaire in Singapore. It was affirmation to my parents in the '90s that the act of migration was worth it. The maintenance on this house was so extreme that if lights went out, they would stay out for months. The white paper lanterns in the living room were so high that for my entire life there, in the thirty-odd years my parents had the house, they never changed the paper lantern shades once. These shades became off-white, moth-eaten globes like the moon would look if it was held against a white sky, but even these lanterns outlived my father. They must have spent every penny they had on this place and didn't calculate the expensive cost of handymen in Australia because the house started going downhill from the day it was bought.

By 2013 this huge house was literally filled with things. I just thanked God that the ceilings were high, and she could still breathe in the communal areas as a result. There were troublingly strange things to collect, like bolts of quilting fabric and cheap shoes from discount stores. My mother would fill one room with these things until it was bursting like trying to roll a sleeping bag back into its impossibly tight sheath. If she couldn't sleep in a room anymore, she would pull out her mattress and move into the next room, and then the next room, like a hermit crab changes its shell. Here was her unraveling illustrated in piles of stuff, a topographic map of disconnection from the world. This process continued until that day where she had failed to show up for dinner and was found lying at the bottom of the shower.

The cleaning went on for five months until I got to ground zero, where all the disconnection began, my mom and dad's master bedroom, where they had slept side by side for thirty-five years. Where she had locked herself in during my childhood for consecutive afternoons. Where she had drenched pillows in her tears after Dad's death. That room.

CONTAINERS FULL OF SADNESS

I'm small. Just five foot one. I walked to the door, heart pounding for fear of what I would find in there. The five months preceding had already yielded so much. Pushing the master bedroom door open and looking up through the crack between it and the doorframe, I could see the random things piled high above my head height. Magazines, clothes, shoes. A heavy broken mattress looking like it had been thrown into the sky and left to land wherever. It pinned the door closed against me as I pushed, resisting me. It wanted to keep the room's secrets hidden.

I took a deep breath and told myself, "Simone, no one else can do this but you; this is the last gift you give to your parents." It truly was. So, I started cleaning and got to work. The most sinister things I found were towers of disposable plastic takeout containers. We all laugh because we all know an ethnic lady that keeps these takeaway containers. But my mom wasn't domestic. She maybe cooked five times for us in our whole childhood. My dad though was this incredible Chinese cook. He would make vats of Hokkien mee, a fantastic Singaporean noodle dish teeming with seafood, and then make me go with these same disposable takeaway containers to our neighbors. And I'd say in my thick Aussie accent at the time, "This is really lame, but my dad made noodles." And push the recycled plastic container, still warm with leftovers, across the threshold of their doorway and into the hands of our Australian neighbors, cocking my head to the side like I was too cool to be doing this. That's how we connected with people— through the shared love of food. Food is love for Asians.

And I realized that my mother was keeping those containers for a time that would never come again, for the parties my dad used to cook all those noodles for, wiping beads of sweat from his forehead as he tossed the wok in his polo shirt and slippers. She was waiting for grandchildren she thought would appear one day. Never has a stack of plastic containers been so heavy with meaning. It was this way with many objects I found in the house.

So, I kept cleaning until I got to carpet level. There were three bags. One bag was full of every obituary on my father's death that had ever been written in a newspaper, clipping after clipping after clipping. Another plastic bag was full of his

X-rays, and the third plastic bag was full of every condolence card she had ever gotten consoling her on his death.

And I remember sitting on the carpet and thinking, "From the day he died, April 6, 2004, this poor woman, my mother, had stopped throwing anything away." When we talk about empty nest syndrome, it's deeper than we think. Some mothers like mine fill the hollowness with stuff, hoping it embraces them and distracts from the emptiness of missing their children.

I recently called my mom for the work I do on human connection and asked her, "What was it like, Mum, after I left for Dubai and Tamara and I grew up?"

"It was like my world crumbled. I would go out to the shops and buy things, cheap things, but at least I could talk to people there," she admitted.

THE BATHTUB THAT BROKE ME

Cleaning a bathtub was what finally broke me mentally; it pushed me to my knees both literally and metaphorically. This bathtub had long been clogged with dark standing water and shopping receipts floating on top of it. I took another deep breath and sighed, saying to myself again, "No one else is going to do this but you; this is the last gift you give your parents." I slapped on the rubber glove and plunged my hand into the water to take the plug out. And that is a moment I'll never forget because every time I do dishes now with rubber gloves on and can feel the water, I am taken back to this moment.

This is the moment that I lost any remaining self-connection. Only six months before, I had been a creative, creating radio shows and writing interviews or launching social media campaigns, but I was now a full-time cleaner, and there is absolutely nothing wrong with that. It's good honest work, but it wasn't what I specialized in or was trained for. In that moment, hearing the sound of the water gurgling out of the tub, I forgot who I was. I had no healthy human connection in my life besides visits to the nursing home to see Mom. My identity dissolved into my gloves in that sludgy black bathtub and didn't emerge again for another half a decade. I had become totally isolated from other people by the act of cleaning the hoard.

LONELINESS CREATING MORE LONELINESS

As Dr. Coan and that *New York Times* article describe, loneliness creates a social awkwardness, a yearning to be around others but a retreating, as well as a holding of others to unreasonably high standards. I remember when this started happening within me. I started by finding reasons not to connect with new people. I told myself there was no other thirty-year-old with a father in the grave and a mother in a wheelchair. I used this falsehood to hold other people to a ridiculously high standard, assuming they could never empathize with me on first meeting. If I went to buy a loaf of bread, I would tell the lady at the bakery my whole life story. I was that thirsty for connection. Oversharing is a form of social awkwardness and a symptom of loneliness.

Brené Brown powerfully states, "We have to own our story and share it with someone who has earned the right to hear it."

The last part is crucial. Oversharing is vulnerability before trust is established.

Another symptom of my loneliness was misreading social cues. I would have rageful outbursts to ethnic aunties visiting my mom's nursing home wielding old-world platitudes about their friends who had strokes and how their Lord, Jesus Christ, saved them. *They didn't have the intel I had,* I thought. I knew what the doctors said. I raged against their opinions and interferences. I had no compassion for their well-intended, hollow messages.

I started painting at home alone and drinking Moscato at noon. I yearned to be invited out to dinner with people my own age, but the extension of an invite yielded stress. I was immediately scared about whether I would say something inappropriate. Could I keep a lid on my crazy? I was so out of practice socializing that, once there, I immediately wanted to withdraw and be alone on the rare occasion I was out.

If these symptoms can happen to me, one of the most social people you'll ever meet, it can happen to absolutely anyone, and COVID-19 and its social distancing means our social skills will atrophy, but like a muscle, we can flex them and get them back. So, here are some connection challenge points we can put into action to cope with the "social recession," as Dr. Coan terms it.

SHARE MORE DEEPLY.

Talk about deeper things among your existing friends and family. In the near future, as described at the beginning of this chapter, where we will be circulating among our existing connections, we have to connect more authentically to get the connection we need.

SPEAK YOUR TRUTH.

Speaking truthfully doesn't just mean telling your story; it also means being transparent. Speaking transparently can help others in your intimate circle know where you are emotionally and connect with you authentically. Try this week to answer honestly when asked "How are you?" by an existing connection.

WHERE YOU CAN, MAKE NEW CONNECTIONS WITH NEW PEOPLE.

We get dopamine, the reward hormone, every time we do something pleasurable like eating chocolate, hugging a puppy, or making new connections. They could be your barista; they could be a new neighbor who has moved in next door. Acknowledge them, give them that oxytocin-inducing eye contact. This is also supported by a study by Julianne Holt-Lunstad at Brigham Young University that calls this type of connection "social integration" and the number one factor in living longer.[20] Having interactions with a hobby group, speaking to and being seen by your neighbors, or even how many people you talk to during the day all help your mental and physical well-being.

TOUCH YOUR LOVED ONES MORE.

In the simulation earlier in this chapter, I mentioned the custom-built wide hallways where employees would not brush shoulders. Oxytocin is not just the social bonding hormone; it's also the touch hormone. We need it. Social distancing threatens to deprive us of our quota long term. So, within your homes, hug your children more, hold your partner's hand, make a concerted effort to do more of it. Make it a challenge to embrace your family this week.

CHAPTER 6

FORGIVE

The Power of Apologizing in Relationships

I didn't grow up in a house that said "sorry." After some of my mom's most blistering menopausal outbursts or what I now think could have been symptoms of her disease—which as a child were first met by my terror but later with contempt as a teenager—there was never a "sorry." Arguments with my father where she fought dirty were never met with an apology, only him storming out red-faced to drive his car alone along the West Coast Highway and returning hours later, calm. My father knew something about the power of words or actions you can never take back. Of course he did; his own father had been an alcoholic, and he had grown up with so much trauma. It always seemed to me that when he turned on his heel, still in his work clothes, exhausted after a long day to exit the house again for relief, he made this conscious decision as a gift to us kids. So we would not have to unhear any more shouting or meanness. I loved him for this, but I also now realize he buried that rage, his emasculation, deep inside him for decades and later emerged with stage IV cancer that began in his kidneys. That's what unresolved rage creates, a disconnection between you and the words you want to say and the feelings you need to get out; your body corrodes. In the words of Louise Hay, "Dis-ease became disease."

I even remember when my sister and I fought, hurt each other, clawed at each other as kids. My parents never did that American TV thing, making us stand facing them in the living room and say "sorry" to each other. I thought hard about it in writing this chapter and realized that any thoughts about apologizing must have been implanted by foreign media. It wasn't just how we fought; it was that we often threw below-the-belt punches. Name-calling and put-downs at the things that we knew would hurt the other person deeply. This acidic tongue protected me in high school and when I entered the media industry, but it's also what surfaces when I am at the lowest integration of myself, when I am tired and agitated. It's as if, once meanness passes your lips, you never get that innocence back.

HOW I FINALLY LEARNED TO APOLOGIZE

The woman who taught me to apologize is someone nameless. I mentioned this story in our introduction. Her hair had slight gray flecks; it flicked out at the side in a long pixie crop. Her voice had a thick South African accent. I was working during my university days at that same sports store I mentioned in earlier chapters. I must have been way too social at this job because I forgot to remove the security tags when I went to scan her clothes at the cash register. During my usual weekly shift, I remember being behind the counter at the back of the store and seeing a woman come in. She looked familiar, swinging her bags with our large logo on them between the racks of clothes. She stormed up to the counter and whacked the bag on the table. I heard the clank of the plastic security tags at the same time. I knew what I had done. She started to remove the clothes, her angry hands trembling, and mumbling, "You left these tags on my clothes. I don't have time for this. I don't have time for this."

Having now grown into an adult, I realize that life in Singapore and Dubai is made easier for us because we can hire domestic help, and how this contrasted with the one and a half years I returned to Perth for Mom. I now fully see why she was so stressed, the amount of time that people lose running a household, cleaning and ferrying kids to school on top of their work without help. I can now fully empathize with this woman's exhaustion. At the time, however, as a child who had a messy house and what I perceived as a mother who didn't clean or ferry us anywhere, all I remember was feeling my heart sink to the pit of my stomach as I recognized the garments and knew it was me.

I saw her receipt with my login name on it, the serif font screaming my name and searing the mistake into me, turning me red-faced. I, of course, said I was sorry, but I think this apologizing I did with my non-Asian friends was almost sociopathic. It was said because I knew it was culturally appropriate. Without ever seeing the deep healing value in the apology, I apologized not because I grasped the huge inconvenience this was to her, the time it took away from her parenting, or the stress it caused her. No, I apologized like a chicken so that I wouldn't get in trouble. Her anger also seemed to diffuse my guilt around this; her anger made me more worried than remorseful.

She grabbed the clothes, and just as quickly as she had stormed into the store, she began storming out. But just before she exited, she paused midstride, turned back on her heels, and walked up to me. I was hiding now behind a rack of clothes, pretending to neaten them. The lady made a beeline for me behind that rack of clothes. Stopped and looked at me, placed her hand on my shoulder, almost teary-eyed, and said, "Look, I am really sorry for getting angry at you. It's just been a really bad day."

I looked directly into this woman's eyes and saw that rare thing we can never really see in social media videos and pictures. Sincerity. I finally saw it, exactly what a sincere apology looks like, how it felt and resonated through my body. Immediately, all of the stress and fear I was feeling dissolved. My hands on that rack stopped trembling.

A sincere apology is one of the greatest tools you can have for healing disconnection in your most treasured relationships. You're not always apologizing because you did something wrong. Of course, if you have, then you should. You're not apologizing for yourself or the space you take up, and we'll discuss this more in a moment. You're apologizing for any hurt that you might have caused to the person. This lady who was my customer did not do anything wrong, I was at fault, but she was apologizing to me because she might have hurt me. Sometimes our greatest teachers are not our parents or people we know. They are people who come into our lives for reasons only the universe has designed.

Apologizing and I have had a more tumultuous and long-term relationship than most of my actual romantic relationships. There were years between when I was full of rage, where I was the woman in the shop. We had swapped places, and I forgot to be the child who learned this lesson. I waged war on myself and everyone around me. I hurt many and didn't say "sorry" because I was engulfed in a battle being waged in my head. Still, it took moving back to Singapore in 2015 and being embedded in a workplace whose dynamics reminded me of my upbringing to make the importance of apologizing stand front and center in my life again. I found that "sorry" was also, like the household I grew up in, not as culturally embedded as in the West.

ALLERGIC TO THE WORD "SORRY"

Recently, at a Michelin-starred French restaurant in Singapore, I was given a glass straw with the previous users' gunk literally still inside it. Sitting in my Coke. The waitress replaced it, but the word "sorry" was never uttered. No apology at all. At my former workplace, rife with politics and backstabbing of the level we're used to seeing in Chinese imperial dramas, I was the new concubine in the palace. This meant I was fair game for bias, snide, antiforeigner comments mumbled by the senior presenters and double-standard rules like being made to do extra work when others weren't. My boss would shame me on the office group chat for an on-air mistake while I was still live on the air, making sure she could twist the knife in deep while listening to my show at the same time to see if it affected me. Everything was so underhanded that it shocked me because I am dangerously comfortable being transparent and honest, as we can see from this book.

I later learned that people rarely said what they actually meant in these sorts of work environments—the meaning was between the lines. Apologizing and specifically using the word "sorry" was taken as an admission of guilt. I was punished for using what my value system told me was an appropriate apology. If I sincerely made a mistake or thought I offended someone, I would apologize. Then an email would be cc'd to almost half of the HR department. I thought to myself many times as the mechanics of the place unveiled itself, *Wow, I should never have emailed sorry for something so small.* Apologies were thought of and treated like you were admitting you were incompetent, and this mistake held crushing disciplinary consequences, mostly consisting of public shaming. By the time two years had passed, I remember thinking, *You must get out of here before you are changed forever by this place.*

So, it's no wonder that no one conceded with an apology when a mistake was made. The body language of guilt and sometimes remorse was there, but the words were never uttered, much like my mother after her outbursts. Sometimes food was given in its place. Buying us a cake because the word "sorry" was like an allergy. After posting about this on social media, so many commented, "This is amazing. I am so glad to have heard this, and it really is an eye-opener and shifts certain ideologies of how sorry/apologizing has always been used this entire time. Thank you." Or, "I've learned something so important from this. Sorry is not always an admission of incompetence. It's also a recognition of the other person's feelings and dignity. Thanks, Simone." Or, "As Asians battle, we never say sorry."

REMORSE

When I was a child at school, a picture book was given to us at age seven called *The Meanies*. In the book, a group of rather terrifying-looking trolls doles out mean behavior to people in their community. After closing the book, my third-grade teacher looked up at us and said, "What the Meanies didn't have was remorse. Remorse is that feeling after you've done something, and you feel bad because you know you shouldn't have done it."

I knew the exact feeling she was speaking about. This is how I first came to identify remorse and later guilt and how it feels in my body. It'll feel different for you. When you feel remorse or guilt, it may be in your gut like me, or it could be in your lower back or even in your brain base. What's important is that you know it when you feel it and take action on it if needed.

APOLOGIZING CONNECTS US

When we say "sorry," we build deeper connections with family and friends because it is risky. That risk and exposure make it an act of vulnerability, and vulnerability truly connects. We are not guaranteed forgiveness or that our apology is accepted simply by saying "sorry." The lack of pride it takes to apologize demonstrates that we value the connection over our own ego. All connection deepens off vulnerability. An apology is like scar tissue; it sits over a wound and allows it to close over and heal. It can be seen on our skin like a reminder, like the word "sorry" hangs in the air between you and that person you love. We remember and are grateful to the people who apologized for hurting us. It connects us.

"Sorry" is one of the most powerful things you can say to the people you love to diffuse hurt and bring harmony back. In a *Harvard Mental Health Letter* article titled "Learning How to Say, 'I'm Sorry'," apologies are described as "a prerequisite for forgiveness," and forgiveness is key to healing and maintaining healthy human connections.[21] I think any of us who want to live peaceful lives have forgiven many people for hurting us without an apology being verbalized. I think that's helpful too, but when there are active connections in our orbits that we want to nurture and maintain, having a good sincere "sorry reflex" can serve us well. It is simply needed to maintain connections, like watering a plant when the soil gets too dry.

If we know all of this, why is apologizing so difficult for us? Apologizing is nothing short of terrifying. TERRIFYING because it is one of the actions in our lives that requires a huge amount of vulnerability because acceptance of your apology is never guaranteed. The reason apologies are so healing is also because of this same vulnerability. When someone makes themselves sincerely vulnerable to us, it's a gift. I describe it as ripping your heart out and placing it on a silver platter on the floor between you and another person, hoping they don't step on it. This is why truly apologizing is so scary. We lose the psychological safety we are wired to crave as human beings, but it is so worth doing if you treasure your human connections.

Now that you know how it works and why it makes you feel that way, I hope it diffuses some of the sting of doing it. Here are my connection challenges.

APOLOGIZE TO OTHERS WITH SINCERITY.

A sincere apology is not sarcastic. Dr. Aaron Lazare, an expert on apologies, says, "Good apologies can foster healing, but a bad apology only makes a bad situation worse."[22]

An apology prefaced by "I am sorry you feel that way" doesn't validate our involvement in the hurt caused but rather gaslights the other person into feeling they only perceived the hurt. It's a terrible way to add fuel to the fire.[23]

DISCERN WHO THE PEOPLE ARE IN YOUR TRIBE WHO MAY NEED AN APOLOGY FROM YOU.

Here's a quick exercise to reveal people you may need to apologize to. Scroll through the most frequently used messaging app on your phone. Look at each person's name and think of them. If you arrive at a person's name where you stop and feel some energy that is not so positive, it may be a sign you need to offer an apology. I want you to really go deep. Close your eyes and think of how you feel each time you have interacted with this person. Have you maybe had a disagreement, an angry email, or a harsh word to them in the past? Now it's time to take ownership over the unsaid apology, that thing that hangs in the air like an open wound. I have reached out and done this a few times in my life to people who deserved an apology; it's scary but so worth it. Do know that not everyone will respond or accept it, but if you're still in contact with them, the probability is quite high that they will.

RECOGNIZE WHEN YOU DON'T NEED TO SAY "SORRY."

Boundaries for apologizing are just as important as apologizing. Just like we don't have to connect with everyone all the time to be good human connectors, we also don't have to apologize for every single thing we do or for the act of being ourselves. In 2015, in the wake of therapy, as the process wore me down and recalibrated me, I hadn't secured my boundaries yet. Everything was in flux. As a result of this, I let many people into my life I wouldn't now and tolerated unbelievably bitchy behavior from people I wouldn't now. I was apologetic for everything, including just being me. I look back at some of the nasty people during that time, and I know with assuredness that I do not owe them an apology and that we are better off not being in one another's orbits. This includes family, which is really difficult for me to say as an Asian woman. I was conditioned to tolerate everything from bitchiness, verbal abuse, and harsh gossip from aunties, cousins, and more. After therapy, the breaking down and building myself back up, I now have really clear boundaries. Think about your own relationship boundaries. Do you find yourself apologizing just for being you?

MAKE REPARATIONS IF NEEDED.

Look at the ways the hurt was caused. If the hurt caused may have been meant to embarrass or cause shame, then apologize to restore dignity and any hurt. But if there has been some sort of loss or damage to property, there needs to be additional reparations. If you scraped another parent's car at the schoolyard, then apologizing for it plus offering to pay for the damage comes across as more sincere.

The best way to begin approaching an apology is by looking at the offense. Is the apology worded in a way that reflects the offense? For example, infidelity in a partnership would see the wording of the apology with a tone that marks the gravity of the offense. You wouldn't use the same language to apologize for leaving the toilet seat up as you would for cheating on your spouse. Eye contact, body language, and emotion (we'll talk about that more in a coming chapter) all communicate remorse just as powerfully as words. Following the apology, there would be steps to remedy the behavior. Here's an example in the case of a cheating spouse: "I know I cannot take back what I have done. It was terrible. I am so sorry. I am committed now to being here at home, focusing on our time together, and seeing a couples therapist with you."

By apologizing in the right way and focusing on providing healing for the person we have hurt, we can more comprehensively maintain the health of our most valued relationships.

CHAPTER 7

RAPPORT

Building Connection by Meeting People
Where They Are

T he news agency in which my father worked seven days
a week for almost twenty years secured us our resi-
dency in Australia and provided us with school fees, holidays
to Singapore, and that very exchange trip to Switzerland that
changed my entire worldview. In the '90s, a time when people
still needed stationary, I loved watching my father serve his
customers. During school holidays, I would be sent to shadow
my dad in the shop. My mother thought if I learned to count
back change manually, I would become better at math in
school. What she didn't count on was the fact my dad was
deeply compassionate.

The minute we would hear the beads of gravel crunch
under the tires of my mother's car after reversing out of the
shopping center parking lot, my dad would allow me to step
back from the counter, stop working, and read all the outdated magazines he would keep. I would sit cross-legged on
the carpet behind his counter surrounded by piles of *Smash
Hits* and *Archie* comics, devouring the content. Ironically, as

we now know, this would not be the last time I would be surrounded by piles of magazines taller than my head height.

On these blissful magazine sorting afternoons, as a nine-year-old, I would get bored of reading after a few hours, and then I would look up and observe my dad serving his customers. His news agency, also prophetically, was opposite a nursing home. I would watch older adults on scooters zip over to buy scratch tickets. These people had the most incredible stories, many of them migrants or even orphans brought to western Australia to work when they were young. I knew these stories because my parents would listen to the elderly when the shop was slow, providing social interaction for them and a place to spend a couple of dollars. It was my father's incredible knack for building rapport almost instantly that primed his customers, making them feel safe to engage in self-disclosure and vulnerability. After my father's death, we found he had given many of these people unlimited tabs that were never paid when they passed away. He truly loved people, and that love was underpinned by empathy and compassion.

I remember watching how he would open an interaction every time a new customer came in. I would look up and see my father standing at the counter. Every time I think of him, I just think of the word "humble." In fact, the only time he wasn't, the only time he exhibited something else in his character, was in the wake of his cancer diagnosis. Here he was enraged, not because that was his personality but because he was pissed off at the universe for not allowing him to stay longer.

When I say my dad was characterized by the word "humble," it's because he wore his humble beginnings in the way he carried himself. Shoulders turned slightly down and inwards. Even though Australia was a fresh start, where new migrants could wipe the slate of their background clean, and no one would know how you were raised, he still had this body language that did not want to take up space. Or maybe it was because my mother seemed to be the opposite, bordering on haughty to those who did not know her brilliance. Maybe he was just trying to balance them out as a couple. Slight in build and not tall, my father always dressed in formal slacks despite the warm Australian weather with a belt with the letter "H" embossed on the buckle. This belt is the one possession of his I have taken all around the world with me to remember him by. It was certainly no Hermes; it simply stood for "Heng."

I would listen intently to what my father would say to his customers, who would profoundly vary in age and background. He would honor them by always talking about the things they wanted to talk about. If a new Malaysian migrant customer came in, my father would lean deep into his hips, giving off a casual air, and thicken his Asian accent. The switch almost said, "I know I have been in Australia over a decade, I know I have raised my family here, but I am still like you, my Asian brother." Then the two would all-out debate which country had the best laksa, Singapore or Malaysia. Then, like a switch, as decisive as traffic lights turn from red to green, if a European customer came in, a German migrant who had been in Australia for two decades, my father would neutralize his accent, mirror the man's upright posture, and talk about the Eurovision song contest. God, we loved Eurovision! My father neutralizing his accent was not an attempt to put on airs or to negate his Asian-ness. Rather it was a simple attempt to be understood more quickly through clarity of communication and this expedited connection. In so doing, he made it far less work for his customers to connect with him. Then when a British customer came in, my father would keep his accent neutral and talk at length about the English Premier League and break down the match play by play. I often wondered why he would allow me to stay up later in the Aussie winter and crack chestnuts in bed watching these matches. My father was a golf fan himself; it's what he played, so it was strange to me to make this effort to watch football also. He was doing it to make sure he always had content to connect with his customers because he knew those customers kept the chestnuts in my hands, the rice bowl in my stomach, and the private school uniform on my back.

Over the years, regular customers, like his British one, came to trust my father deeply because of his consistent choice to be of service in his communication. He would, in a sense, inconvenience himself, his need to talk about whatever he wanted to talk about, in the language or accent of his preference, to make others feel served. To make others feel welcomed and have their stories validated. I learned quickly that true connection happens when others feel seen and heard. These small tweaks in communication allowed my dad's customers to perceive him as one of them, a member of their tribe. Once rapport was established, he built trust by consistently showing up in this way over the course of decades. The rapport my father built created a deep trust, which allowed long-term connection to happen.

I also realized that watching my dad serve customers, pivoting his communication, learning the interests of others, and neutralizing his accent subconsciously became the backbone of my broadcasting career. In my fifteen years in radio, I worked on the mic for stations in Dubai, Australia, and Singapore. To this day, I don't know any other radio DJ in the world who has done that because radio is a notoriously local medium. It prides itself on its insularity. So, I effectively had been paid to persuade people in three hugely diverse markets that I could speak to their heartbeat and to serve their interests. I learned this from my dad.

Almost exactly a decade after those school holidays sitting in the shop and watching, beads of gravel once again crunched under the tires of a car in that shopping center parking lot. This time the car was the hearse carrying my father's body on the morning of his funeral. We had decided to drive my father's daily routine before finally ending up at the church for the service. I remember it being a cold morning, pressing my cheek against the cool glass of that car window, and looking out to see a sea of people, some of them bank employees from the bank where my dad put his float in for the day, dressed in their fresh workday outfits; the pharmacist wearing black to pay respects; Harry, the Greek man who owned the fish and chip shop, the pallbearer for my dad's casket. And there stood his German customer, his Malaysian customer, his British customer. They showed up for their humble local shopkeeper at the end of his life. This is how I know this approach to connection works.

BUILDING RAPPORT

In his book *The Art of Reading Minds*, author Henrik Fexeus says the basic rule of rapport is to "adapt to how the other person communicates" versus imposing what you want to talk about and how you want to talk about it. Good rapport is magic because it allows people to feel closer to us and eventually be more easily persuaded by our agenda because they like us. This may sound a tad inauthentic to you but let me assure you, in a world that has been socially distanced, a world increasingly polarized, these innate steps of connection that we are actually wired to do naturally need to be signposted to bring us back together.

Here's another analogy for rapport building that may make you see this not as an act of trickery or mimicry but one of humble service. One of the human connection superheroes I interviewed for my TEDx Talk on the power of human connection was a teacher at the leading school for children with autism in Singapore. She mentioned to me that UDL, the universal design for learning (an approach in teaching that advocates for equal opportunity for all students by giving students multiple means of expression of what they have learned and multiple means of accessing material so they can choose what works best for them), helped her connect with her students, regardless of where on the spectrum they were. Instead of a test, students can submit an artistic map of what they learned or deliver a talk. UDL has proven very successful for being a more inclusive way of teaching and connecting with students, effectively allowing them to be met where they are. It's a brilliant analogy for the kind of rapport-building communication my father specialized in, meeting people not halfway but 80 percent of the way, and this is something we can all emulate in a world thirsty for connection.

Here are some connection challenges for building rapport.

USE YOUR BODY TO CONNECT.

Like my father did over the counter, he would mirror the body posture of his customers. This tells the brain of the person you are trying to connect with that "this person is like me." My dad did a great deal of communicating with his body despite being cordoned off by his shop counter. Just like what we experience during virtual conferences today, he only had his upper body to communicate with. Mirroring is also valuable for digital communication; frame the bottom of your laptop screen when on a virtual conference to where your sternum ends. By having your hands in the shot, you build trust with your audience. As humans, we are suspicious of concealed hands (hands behind the back when speaking to a live audience or below a desk when doing virtual presentations). This goes back to our days as early men, where our brains became wired to immediately check that a stranger was not holding a weapon in their hands that could hurt us. Vanessa Van Edwards states in her TEDx Talk *You Are Contagious* that it is exactly because of this survival mechanism that, to this day, the first thing we do when we meet a new person is glance at their hands.[24] So to build trust and connection, frame your virtual screen wider to include your arms and your upper torso.

HARNESS THE POWER OF YOUR VOICE.

If the person is a quiet talker, match their volume level. If they speak a language you speak as well, switch to theirs. If they speak English as a second language and struggle to understand, slow your own speech down. Make it easier for the other person on any level to connect with you more quickly, meeting them more than halfway.

INCONVENIENCE YOURSELF.

Try putting aside your needs to discuss what you want to talk about in initial meetings with a new connection. Just listen, soak up who the person is first, and then connect with them on the topics they prefer where you have some common ground. Eventually, when trust and rapport are established, they should come and ask you more about your likes and loves too.

BE ON THE LOOKOUT FOR THINGS TO CONNECT ON.

I often get asked how to connect with a new person in this way if they don't disclose anything about themselves. Great human connectors know that connection leaves clues, so they scan for commonalities constantly. I would often see my dad glance at a customer's attire and see them wearing a cap emblazoned with their favorite sports team's logo. He would then rattle off any trivia he knew about this team or the sport they played to begin the conversation. Prime yourself to look for connection points when you are at your next social gathering or virtual meeting. What clues can you see that you could connect on?

CHAPTER 8

UNMASKED

The Power of Facial Expressions to Connection

I t's 2013 and I stand at a radio panel. "Safe and Sound" by Capital Cities is playing, blasting out of the radio speakers. My eyes are watching the radio log on a computer screen, which in itself is like reading a real-time music chart with an electronic list of songs and digital buttons. If you toggle just one of those elements incorrectly, it will make a song end, skip, and even mix two highly recognizable songs together on an unlucky day. I say highly recognizable because the station I am working at in Dubai is a huge brand, and it plays Top 40 hits. The tunes play on repeat until they get inside you, and you find yourself pumping gas nodding your head.

This particular song, still relatively new, is by two Armenian brothers in LA. I am noting this down on paper, prepping in my head to back sell the song after it stops in sixty seconds. "Back selling," I have been taught, is to describe something interesting about the song in retrospect. But then my thoughts are hijacked like a home invader has run into my head and scooped up the entire contents of my brain in his hands and run back out my ear. All I hear is a kind of tinny white noise. I am out of my own body because the otherwise upbeat lyrics and surging medieval horns of the song cannot make peace with what I am feeling inside: "Even if the sky is falling down, I know that we'll be safe and sound, we're safe and..."

This, I now know, is what they call a trigger. Thirty seconds to go before the song stops, I am sobbing because the last thing I feel is "safe" or "sound" or like I'll be okay because my sky IS falling down. I've been back in Dubai for a week after returning from three weeks in Australia following my mom's stroke. That very afternoon, I am going to go in to resign from my dream job of half a decade. This brand I gave my life to. The image of my mother, gray-skinned and terrified, lying at the bottom of the shower, curled inward onto herself like a snail, is all I see. She is all alone. The guilt and shame are unbearable. That stroke, I didn't know then, would lead her to sit in her waste for the rest of her life. Ten seconds. I blow my nose, stand up straight at the panel, and smile my largest, happiest smile because I know people can hear it in my voice. That's what I have been taught. I still believe the smile is to the voice what eye contact is to the face. It primes for connection.

I disconnect my needs, my sorrow, and the fight-or-flight response for just a moment. I tell myself, "It's connection time with others now." Give the audience what they want. That's what I have been conditioned to do my whole adult life. Five, four, three, two, one. The song stops.

"It's 104.4 Virgin Radio Dubai. This is Simone Heng on the Lowdown. Two Armenian brothers out of LA there with their surging lyrics, new to the playlist it's Capital Cities..."

My smile widens so I make it through. I'm rushing the talk break; I know it. I tell my mouth to slow down. I remember this telling because that is what fight-or-flight mode does. It makes conscious and deliberate thought feel like labor. I smile harder until I can feel the stretching of skin in the corner of my mouth. I feel tears formed twenty seconds ago drying on my cheeks. Then I continue. That is my job; that is what I have been programmed to do.

"Coming up next, music from Rihanna, David Guetta, and Jay Sean. You're listening to Virgin," I say.

EMOTION FROM THE OUTSIDE IN

The talk break is over. My chest depresses from being full of air and energy. The skin in the corners of my mouth stretched upward has come back to the place nature intended, curled downwards like deflated birthday balloon rubber. My smile starts to fade again. I am exhausted. The ads are playing, and while they do, I check in with myself, connect with myself. How do I feel? That's where I can see and feel the difference. I feel marginally better. The act of being forced to change my body language and my facial expressions has actually made me feel happier. Tired but happier. I shelve this realization in my library of overwhelming thoughts during a crisis.

Half a decade later, I'll learn at a Tony Robbins conference amid euphoric strangers that that's how it works. That we can change our energy, mental state, and mood simply by altering our physicality. Tony gets the entire twenty-thousand-strong crowd to hunch over and mimic the posture of what we think a depressed person may stand like. Then we mimic how we think a confident person would stand. Then he explains to us the science behind Amy Cuddy's power poses,[25] and I realize just how right he is about this. I've been doing my power poses and teaching my clients how to change their state ever since.[26]

THE ART OF SAVING FACE

Your facial expressions are the physical manifestation of your emotions. The willingness to express and have mastery over your facial expressions is incredibly powerful, not just for changing your state as I have described in my on-air story earlier, but also for connecting with others. On the one hand, changing your face, as I did on air, to induce "happy hormones" into your body can be effective. In that case, it got me through my shift at work that day in that sad moment. But are there negative implications to our ability to connect with others if we constantly repress our emotions and conceal our facial expressions? This is what we'll explore next.

Learning to harness the power of your facial expressions in a COVID-19 mask-wearing world has never been more important. However, where I live, in Asia and as an Asian woman, we were wearing masks long before a pandemic. For thousands of years, East Asian people and particularly East Asian women have been told to be quiet, mitigate our negative and private feelings (soften our expressiveness), and "not give too much away." This results in an almost freezing of the facial expressions, like a culturally infused Botox jab. If we do not express, we do not risk losing our dignity or our family's. What do we give people in its place? We save face. We are taught this from the time we are young because losing face is an almost unbearable insult for many ethnically Chinese people.

As an Asian girl growing up, it would not be unheard of to have my mother or aunties say, "Eh, don't give so much away" and "Be less animated; don't be so crazy." For me, being expressive was soon associated with being less demure and, therefore, undesirable. The act of not emoting for self-preservation means that I learned to equate expressiveness with weakness and to resent the innate expressiveness that has turned out to be the gift of my entire career.

I would be shushed at home but empowered to express my emotions at my Australian school. In fact, to get the grades that my parents wanted in this Australian school, I needed to learn to show emotion in class. This created an almost schizo-phrenic-like code-switching that many Asian children grow-ing up in Western cultures can relate to. At home, we were given approval based on obedience, not expressing an opinion with our mouths or faces. We were commended for not giv-ing too much away about how we felt or what we thought to people outside of our family unit, yet to be understood in the Western context we lived in, we had to learn to express ourselves.

A LACK OF EXPRESSIVENESS CAN AFFECT CONNECTION

When we don't emote fully, we run the risk of losing out on a whole lot of deep, authentic connections for a few reasons. Firstly, people perceive us as less transparent and don't feel safe with us. We also give so little emotional information away that it's hard for people to read us. Through the godfather of mapping facial expressions, Dr. Paul Ekman, we know the interpretation of all but seven facial expressions that differ greatly across cultures.[27] He describes these as universal facial expressions: anger, contempt, disgust, fear, joy, sadness, and surprise. A more recent study in the Trobriand Islands by Bos-ton College Professor of Psychology James A. Russell and col-leagues may have called into question the interpretation of the expression of fear as universal; however, Ekman's work on the other expressions is still valuable here.[28]

When we express emotions fully, it allows other people to connect with us more quickly because they have a temperature gauge for what we are thinking. In my last workplace in Singapore before becoming a full-time speaker, I was constantly confused. Any negative emotions were mitigated, a complete swallowing of facial expressions. So, when I first started, I could never read if someone was mad at me or if I overstepped. I would only find harsh, reprimanding emails later, but a sweet, neutral expression sold to me in person. There is a part of Asian upbringing, the Chinese part of me knows, that values the concealment of information, and this has many benefits, such as negotiating business contracts. However, this doesn't serve us as well connecting in the global context. Post-COVID-19, we are doing business daily with people around the world who are looking at our faces on video conferences and trying to read us.

We have all, regardless of ethnicity, experienced how challenging it has been reading the faces of our fellow humans in their COVID-19-induced masks. A total mitigation of meaning and communication not landing right. One person I know described reading faces with masks on like "reading a heavily redacted text. Feeling like something important gets missed." Studies back up her feelings, indicating that masks inhibit the capability to perceive a lot of social information. Furthermore, they make emotions more difficult to interpret and block facial mimicry and behavioral synchrony, lowering social bonds, empathy, and playful interactions.[29]

The more countries I have lived in and the more international our world becomes, the more I have realized that masking our feelings is a direct route to not connecting authentically. If you conceal your emotions and thoughts constantly, people connect with an avatar of you instead of you. It also means the vulnerability that comes from the expression of emotions on your face is absent, and vulnerability is how we truly connect. When we show emotion, it builds trust because we demonstrate a transparency that tells other people it is safe to connect.

In summary, facial expressions are powerful tools for connection to change our state and connect with others. Here are some connection challenges to start really activating your facial expressions as a tool for human connection.

USE YOUR FACIAL EXPRESSIONS TO IMPROVE YOUR MOOD AND FEELING.

Manipulating your facial expressions as a momentary mood booster is not a wholly bad thing. In the very first story I shared about having to smile on air, even though I felt terrible inside, I was not meeting anyone. I just needed a perk up. If you're having an off day, do some smiling before you go into work or need to perform in a high-stakes meeting. Smiling when you don't feel happy can trick your brain into believing you feel better than you do. Studies have shown that a smile stimulates the production of dopamine, the feel-good hormone, and serotonin, which is a stress reducer. So, there is science behind why we should smile behind our masks during a time of huge anxiety like the COVID-19 pandemic and its aftermath.[30]

FIND OUT HOW EXPRESSIVE YOU ACTUALLY ARE.

Here's a quick self-connection exercise. Take some selfies of the seven universal expressions: anger, contempt, disgust, fear, joy, sadness, and surprise. Then do a Google search and look at the images of the expressions under each of them. Do your selfies match these? How did expressing these feelings feel for you? Is this something you express naturally, or do you find expressing these emotions foreign, like you haven't exercised them since you were a child? Think about when the last time was that you expressed one of these emotions. Was there a feeling of being totally out of control, or was expressing them a relief? Repressing and not expressing negative emotions to our most intimate connections can mean that those we love do not know how we feel and cannot fully support us if we need them.

PRACTICE EXPRESSING WITH YOUR EYES.

Eye contact is imperative to building trust. With the mask-wearing we have been made to do for the pandemic, learning to be comfortable giving eye contact is vital. Human beings are naturally suspicious of people who avert their eye contact. Eye contact also produces the social bonding hormone oxytocin. Make a concerted effort to make eye contact within your household first by looking up from those devices and releasing oxytocin, the feel-good hormone.[31] When smiling behind that mask, make an effort to smile with your eyes, what is called the "Duchenne smile," a smile that crinkles the corners of your eyes and is perceived as sincere by others. It's a great way to connect when wearing a COVID-19 mask.

CHAPTER 9

NOMAD

Learning to Connect from Serial Expatriates

In high school, as a result of what I didn't know at that time to be a limiting belief that I was "unlovable," I would play a game. As a thirteen-year-old, I would see how many people from any grade I could say hello to when we crossed in the hallways. Soon I would see people almost nervous as I approached; they knew I would be acknowledging them. Their faces trying to avert eye contact, not dissimilar from the subtle social awkwardness we have seen on video conferences during the pandemic. This is a great analogy for how connection can feel since the advent of social media. It's surface level, it's broad and shallow, and it's often awkward. It's what Arianna Huffington describes in her Thrive newsletter as a "junk food version of connection" that fails to give us the real emotional sustenance that keeps us healthy and happy.

MANY SUPERFICIAL CONNECTIONS

So what's the kind of connection we actually need? In Susan Pinker's TED Talk, she shares Julianne Holt-Lunstad's research and describes the kind of close relationships we need as "the people that you can call on for a loan if you need money suddenly, who will call the doctor if you're not feeling well or who will take you to the hospital, or who will sit with you if you're having an existential crisis."[32] These are the friendships we should be nurturing as deep connections. When we have a quantity of low-depth human connections, I have found that it simply makes us crave something deeper. A large network is great, provided you also have a bedrock of healthy, quality, intimate connections to support you. In my midtwenties, when I moved to Dubai, I remember attending event after event in that city in a thirst for belonging and because I justified it was great "networking" for my career. I didn't realize that none of this being surrounded by people would heal my longing for belonging because I was experiencing deep intimate and relational loneliness. From the statistics shared in earlier chapters, I believe that a large proportion of the world is also currently searching for more valuable connections.

Christina Sang is a thirty-three-year-old serial expatriate who has lived in the Philippines, France, the United Arab Emirates, Portugal, the US, the UK, and Switzerland. She was most recently stuck in her now-home of Bali for over a year during the pandemic. When living in Dubai, Christina worked in corporate communications for some of the most illustrious hotels. She was also a PR consultant to over a hundred luxury brands in art and culture and select diplomatic events, including taking care of royalty and Hollywood A-listers.

I asked her about her experience in Dubai creating so many events, where surface-level connections take center stage, and how they made her feel. She answered, "I felt like the majority of the people, as I moved my career from hospitality into consultancy and then being in PR representing luxury brands and royalty, always wanted something from me. So, 90 percent of the time, I would speak to people on a day-to-day basis that wanted to use me or needed something from me. So, it becomes a vicious cycle, and the promiscuity of those connections is just too much. It's like you have an energy tank for connection, and all that energy is going into meaningless fluff."

Christina's feelings here of "everybody wanting something from me" was certainly how I felt at times with my work on the radio. Businesses both big and small sidling up to me in the hope I would mention their brands on air, which I absolutely could not do for free anyway; I would have been fired.

There's good science behind why we're wary of such connections. Psychologist and thought leader in the study of loneliness, the late Professor John Cacioppo, says,

> If you look at early humans and other hominids, they were not uniformly positive toward each other. We exploit each other, we punish each other, we threaten each other, we coerce. And so it isn't that I want to connect with anyone, I need to worry about friend or foe... If I mistakenly detect someone as a friend when they're a foe, that can cost me my life. Over evolution, we've been shaped to have this bias....You're motivated to connect. But promiscuous connection with others can lead to death. A neural mechanism kicks in to make you a little skeptical or dubious about connecting.[33]

A LONELY BRAIN MAKES YOU LONELIER

During those "networking" years, my social orbits became swollen. I was surrounded by people, giving me the impression I was less alone, but it never really satiated me. After a big breakup, I soon became steeped in intimate loneliness. I craved a partner badly. Some days the love others were finding was hard for me to celebrate, bringing my own unlovability into stark relief. A self-loathing set in. How could I have dealt with so much suffering in my personal life and this one thing I needed, the universe would not give me? It wasn't rational, but the lonely brain often isn't. It becomes suspicious of everyone, tests friends, and is on high alert for people's betrayal. It becomes a loop. The lonelier you feel, the harder you make it for connection to come into your life.

This is backed by Cacioppo's findings too. The lonely brain becomes hypervigilant to social threats, many times more than the nonlonely brain. I became sensitive. If a friend canceled, I would take it as abandonment. If someone was late to meet, it was a deep sign of disrespect, even if they were really good people who had totally understandable reasons for doing so. I would even be annoyed at every new person who would reach out to connect. If I did meet up with them, I would soon find a fault for why I would not want to connect with them again. This is what the lonely brain does. It's trying to keep you safe but, in the process, makes you more lonely. If you're experiencing this, I write this because I want you to know this is backed by science. You are not alone.

QUANTIFYING CONNECTION

So how many connections should we aim to have? According to evolutionary anthropologist Robin Dunbar, we can only maintain 150 meaningful contacts. Dunbar states,

> The way in which our social world is constructed is part
> and parcel of our biological inheritance....We're mem-
> bers of the primate family—and within the primates

there is a general relationship between the size of the brain and the size of the social group. We (human beings) fit a pattern. There are social circles beyond it and layers within—but there is a natural grouping of 150.[34]

In a world where social media followers and connections give us the feeling of having a limitless tribe, this finding, now termed "Dunbar's Number," allows us to assess not only the number of people in our orbits of connection but also to assess what constitutes a "meaningful contact" in our lives. If you're in that space I was back in my midtwenties in Dubai, this study can really help you audit your human connections. Are you surrounded by a superfluous network that works not to make you feel a deeper sense of belonging but rather makes you feel more alone?

Having lived in cities like Perth and St. Gallen, Switzerland, versus Singapore and Dubai, the lack of transience in the former breeds a different sort of connection, which is interesting to understand and can also set fertile ground for deep loneliness for totally different reasons. Loneliness, as we know, is indifferent to location. You can be anywhere and still be lonely. This is something I felt when I repatriated back to Australia to care for my mother after a decade of being away.

RESISTANCE TO BROADENING ESTABLISHED SOCIAL GROUPS

Nonexpatriate settings see more people retaining their friendships from as early as high school. People in these environments seemingly have all the connections they need; there is a permanence in the orbits of their connection. They've gone deep, not wide, like those of us in those transient expat cities.

There is a lot of value in deep connection but what it also means for those who have had their same tribe for decades, set almost in concrete, is they aren't so keen to start inviting new people in at their dinner parties. It's logical; it's how we are wired in our cavemen brains to keep ourselves safe from the unknown. Upon my repatriation, I became a social threat, rarely invited in or asked to join already established social groups of people my own age. This was so different from how quickly new social connections are tried on for size in expat cities; it literally sent me into a reverse culture shock. The experience for me as a single female was the most socially isolating of my life.

I am not alone in experiencing this. Heather Hansen, a global communications expert who is from the US but has lived as an expat primarily in Singapore and Denmark and did so, unlike me, with both her spouse and children, described the difference between Singapore and moving back to her husband's home in Denmark:

> It's different because in Denmark there isn't the same expat culture. You are pushed into the local culture much faster than in Singapore. There isn't that divide between "expat" and "local" that can be seen in Singapore as well. And of course, since I was married to a Dane and I speak the language, you would think that I would connect quite easily, but I didn't feel that. I have maybe two good friends of my own that are not through my husband here.
>
> I actually found it very difficult because in Denmark, people grow up and make their friends at a very young age. And they're still friends with those people as adults. I love my husband's group of friends, and they have fully accepted me, but still it's usually those

kinds of group things. It's not that I would call one of them with my problems to have a girl chat. We are very much like a group of friends who did things together, not those personal one-on-one connections.

Denmark is pretty closed. I was included in my husband's circle because I was married to the culture. I wouldn't have ever been invited into that group any other way. Primarily because you have your close friends, and you don't really have a need for new friends outside of those circles. I get it, but it does make it very, very difficult to break into a culture.

By now, we know that human beings evolved to value safety in numbers and that people outside the tribe posed a social threat, so it makes sense that we find it hard to let new people in when we feel our social needs are already safely being met. But in the world we now live in, where loneliness is the secret pandemic leading to a mental health crisis, I argue we may have to push past these innate instincts in two distinct ways. Firstly, I hope that those reading this book who feel they have their social connections in place think of ways to challenge themselves to let someone new in. How can you place your own comfort and busyness aside and give your time, even in small ways, to those who feel alone? The rewards of doing so are incredible. A new friend bringing new insights and conversations can be priceless. Secondly, for those of us who are expats, we can learn to harness some of the depth and stability from these nonexpat environments.

LEARNING TO MIMIC THE EXPAT MINDSET

The other side of expatriate cities, like Singapore, Dubai, and Hong Kong, is that people are separated from their families.

To combat the transience of friends leaving constantly, people are much more open to allowing new connections into their fold. This is different from when one permanently migrates to a new place; expats know they will not be there forever. The perception of being a visitor also leads to a feeling of urgency about their time in a particular place, which I did not experience in nontransient environments. The lack of psychological safety one feels as a foreigner compels us to find connection quickly. Remember our brains are always wired for connection and associate safety in numbers. This compels us to find a group of friends to form a safe tribe quickly. This tribe essentially sits in for and substitutes for our friends and family back home. As a result of this, connection is fast and exponential in its nature. You disclose much more about yourself with new people because, frankly, you don't have twenty years to make friends slowly since you're only planning to stay in the place for two.

In a world where social isolation is now headline news, I argue that we can learn a lot from how people connect when they live a serial expatriate lifestyle. We can harness a bit of this bravery born of urgency to go out and connect regardless of where we live.

USE COMMONALITIES TO CONNECT.

One of Christina Sang's favorite techniques to connect with others when she lived in Portugal as a foreigner who couldn't speak any Portuguese is what I call "commonalities that connect." "I just found a point of resonance or a point of relatability. I would literally be like, 'Oh, well, you and I like food; all right, let's start from there. Let's start the basis of friendship building from there.' I would go out clubbing, I'd meet some girls I don't know in the bathroom and ask, 'Let's catch up and exchange numbers,'" she said. This week, use Christina's technique of finding commonalities that connect. Look for people in your day-to-day routine or when out. Scan them visually. What physical commonality may they have as a point to start a conversation? The same leather jacket you own at home? A sports tee from your favorite team? Condition yourself to see the similarities over differences and then harness that expat bravery and strike up a conversation.

AUDIT YOUR EXISTING CONNECTIONS.

Look at your existing group of connections. Are there people in the group who make you feel less connected? What bonds you as a group? Do you share deeply, or do you feel you can never get anything beyond superficial conversation? It may be time to refine who you surround yourself with, making space for new people to come in.

LET IN A NEW TRIBE MEMBER.

Are there people in your workplace or city who may be new? One thing that I loved about my parents was that they would always invite foreign students from nearby Murdoch University to our table. They knew what it felt like to be alone in a new country as immigrants themselves. It was so enriching for us as young children to learn about places we had never traveled to. Who could you create space for at your table?

CHAPTER 10

SERVE

Service as an Antidote to Loneliness

As a child from birth until age seventeen, when I went to live in Switzerland, I attended church service every Sunday. It is during the mass that I was told over and over again about the power of giving to others. It is one thing to be a sassy fourteen-year-old sitting in a pew listening to this. It is another thing entirely to feel the true, profound connecting power of serving others.

As I gazed out the window of the same church building I would later eulogize my father in, I would see older migrant ladies, many of them what we call Asian "aunties" preparing busily in the church cafeteria. Removing delicately placed cling wrap from the sides of Pyrex dishes, inside of which were homemade curry puffs and tea cakes nestled in paper towels. I would look longingly at this, willing the priest to close the mass so we could run out and get some of those treats. Dad would give me his spare change to buy things, and with a sweaty palm heavy with huge Australian fifty-cent coins, I would skip over the grass courtyard to the canteen.

People would stay behind after mass to chat while nibbling on their purchases, golden light streaming in on their shoulders as they jostled for the priest to come over and speak to them.

What I remember most profoundly was the passion with which these older women, their children long grown up and living in other cities like Melbourne and Sydney, would serve us. The money from these bake sales they painstakingly prepared would go toward building something new in the church or helping a charity beyond the community. They would take my change and nestle clean, white napkins in my hand before placing a bright green sweet popiah called a Kuih Dadar in one or a crisp curry puff in the other. In the background, I would see that this small canteen was full of ladies of all colors— Indian, White Australian, East Asian, and Italian—swinging tea towels around their shoulders as they wiped down borrowed trays and cutlery ready to return to their owners. This is when I truly saw how powerful connection born of service could be. The simple act of putting out some food unified the families who stayed behind at mass to connect. It unified the women by creating friendships, and this made me see the power of connection far more profoundly than any sermon could. It was not religion that was actually connecting people in this scenario; it was the power of serving. The women were serving a greater charitable cause by baking and being in that canteen on their otherwise leisurely Sunday. My father was serving me with change from his earnings, and I was serving my family the treats I purchased so they could stand in that courtyard conversing with the priest uninterrupted. We were all putting our egos aside to be of service to others in some way. Being intertwined in service is one of the keys to feeling healthily socially connected.

WHEN SERVING IS YOUR JOB

But what happens when service is your job and you need to maintain the energy to show up for others daily? Kanitha catches the MRT (our version of the subway train) all over Singapore every day to make home visits for people who are struggling. When she isn't traveling between locations, she sits at her desk anticipating walk-ins—overwhelmed people who can no longer cope. When they finally decide to reach out for a helping hand, it's not at a time that can be prebooked. They urgently need to connect with someone, and it's Kanitha they go to.

She has been a social worker for six years and decided to become one after her own sister died at the age of seven. Kanitha yearned for a role model or a mentor as her family dealt with the trauma of the loss. She vowed when she grew up to ensure that others who felt forgotten, alone, or unsure of how to cope with their own trauma could get help through her. Kanitha describes her day-to-day life:

> On a daily basis, most social workers have to deal with the most vulnerable and dark sides of human nature. One day a client came in expressing really openly that she wanted to kill herself. All I did was spend an hour with her—and I allowed her that space and time to share about the problems in her life, and she cried her heart out. At the end, she left feeling a lot lighter and even shared that just being able to have this conversation gave her faith that she could endure and continue the fight. I knew that that one conversation did impact her, and just knowing she had this lifeline that she could reach out to anytime instead of feeling alone and cut off from the world gave her the consolation and confidence to manage things on her own.

Part of what makes Kanitha's work so powerful, and something that we can all harness in our own lives, is that the kind of connection that makes people feel they truly belong is comprised of communication where they feel seen, heard, and understood fully without judgment.

CONNECTING TO THE TRIBE THROUGH ACTS OF SERVICE

Kanitha's life in service of others taps into something that has come up again and again in my research on human connection: giving to others makes us feel more connected to the tribe. When we were early man living in tribes, our worst fear was to be cast out. What better way to solidify your place in the tribe than to be useful to it, to positively impact it to such a level that you become indispensable. When we contribute to something bigger than ourselves, we feel more secure and connected. Therefore, being of service also gives us a greater sense of psychological safety. When we can impact our community positively, it's a reminder that we matter. If you're experiencing collective loneliness—a feeling of disconnection from a group with a like-minded purpose—then being of service could also be a way to find people with similar values and mindsets. You can make friends while helping others. It's a wonderful ecosystem of connection.

But being of service isn't, of course, just about making ourselves feel better; it's about actually helping other people. Shelly Tygielski is the founder of Pandemic of Love, a global, grassroots, volunteer-led, formalized mutual aid community. "Mutual aid" is a voluntary reciprocal exchange of resources and services, based on the principle that members of a community should feel responsible for caring for one another and aspire to develop a community safety net where no individual goes hungry, without shelter, or feeling alone. The entire organization centers on volunteers doing good for others, using Pandemic of Love only as mediators to match them with other people in need. It's a special project because people donating their time, services, and money are in direct contact with the people they are helping, so they can see the positive impact they are making in the community. This makes both the giver and recipient of aid feel more connected. This was Shelly's response when I asked how she sees people change through being of service to others:

> Connection is not a one-way street. In order for a connection to occur, two people need to lean in and make it happen. They have to be willing, vulnerable, and open to working through any obstacles or challenges that may arise, understanding that the outcome will ultimately be worth it. What I have witnessed through the connections made through Pandemic of Love is the fact that the emotional well-being of the individual being helped is affected just as much as the well-being of the donor assisting that person. Why? Because as much as it makes the recipient feel seen and heard, as well as obtain a measure of financial relief, it also makes the donor feel useful, capable of enacting change, and empowered to make a difference. I have witnessed how people who have signed up to be a donor and then truly committed to creating an authentic connection with the person/family they are matched with are forever changed.[35]

We instinctively know doing good deeds for others feels good, but it's also really useful in extracting us from our own sense of isolation. Service is an antidote for loneliness. It pulls the lonely brain out of self-preservation, offering perspective. In giving to others, we receive. It has been said a million times before but may need reminding in the world in which we currently live. A life of success without service to something beyond ourselves eventually becomes hollow.

SERVE PEOPLE THE WAY *THEY* WANT TO BE SERVED

When we serve others, there is also an inconvenience to ourselves that allows others to be more comfortable. As I mentioned in the chapter on rapport, I saw this while watching my father communicate with his customers. He would connect with them how they preferred. Kanitha sees this in her own work:

> People always say treat others how you want to be treated, but I often wonder, why do we not treat people how they want to be treated? It's important to be mindful of what brings them comfort; because something entirely different could give you comfort... So pace with them. Journey with them. Don't try and fix someone on your own timeline. Allow them to go through their grief, allow them to go through their struggles and then let them grow from it.

Vivian Pei is a food and beverage consultant, raised in the US by Chinese parents. Viv is a service-industry veteran who started waiting tables in her father's restaurant at age fourteen. She bussed tables, hostessing and waitressing all the way through to working in restaurants' kitchens in France. She experienced the thrill and joy of making others happy through service and serving them the way they love to be served on a daily basis:

I was working at CÉ LA VI as a guest chef and one of the waitstaff comes into the kitchen fifteen minutes before last orders and says, "Please tell me we have something vegan on the menu because we have these customers come in saying we have to feed them and all five of them are vegan." As a cook, instead of just telling them to get lost, I just said let's look at what we can do for them. So, I looked at the menu that was there and the ingredients that we had, and we figured it out. We made them a very good meal…One of the biggest joys for me being front of house is to serve a guest in a way that makes them feel really happy. Sending someone off with a smile on their face. I mean that makes me feel good.

There is so much we can learn from people who work serving others. Just look at our healthcare workers during the COVID-19 crisis! Yes, it is their paid job, but this joy from sacrificing for and helping other people lights them up in a special way that may not exist in those of us who don't work in service. I see this in the deep reservoirs of patience that my mother's caregivers in the nursing home have. How can we infuse the joy of a service attitude into our lives, knowing that it helps fend off isolation, adds to our sense of purpose, and makes us feel good in the process?

Service isn't just about the time we take to show up and do a charity project, and it isn't the sacrificing of money in a donation. It's challenging ourselves to be others-driven in a self-serving world and infusing that mindset into how we think about communicating and connecting everywhere.

VOLUNTEER OR DO SOMETHING GOOD FOR OTHERS.

As we now know, volunteering and doing good deeds are fantastic ways to make yourself feel less lonely, and it empowers you. Have a look in your local community to see where you could volunteer your time. Choose something that appeals to your unique interests and talents, and you'll find the opportunity to make new friends more likely as well. Having a group of friends to volunteer with will make it more likely you'll regularly contribute as well.

SHARE YOUR STORY AND SEE IT SERVE.

I was part of school programs at homeless shelters and Indigenous women's homes as a young teen. I never realized how soothing being of service could be because I wasn't lonely then. The gap between myself and the people I was serving was palpable. I felt awkward, steeped in my own privilege. How could I relate to the trauma and abuse these women had felt in my middle-class, suburban home?

However, my father died as I grew into life, and Mom got ill. I now feel we would have had much more to connect on. Certain things, like trauma, grief, and loss, are universal human experiences, and in some ways, these hardships are gifts because they provide such fertile ground for connection. Kanitha sees this in her own work:

> Sometimes it's difficult to convince people that there is a reason behind your suffering and your pain. I do believe in vulnerability. I believe that clients will only trust us when they know we understand their pain. Where appropriate I do share my own stories and experiences just to show that I am not on a pedestal. We all are humans here; we all have our own suffering.

Sit down and reflect. What stories do you have that can be used to connect with others? What were times in your life where you were hurting and it took superhuman strength to get back up? Add these moments to your connection tool kit.

CHAPTER 11

PARADOX

Forging Authentic Connection in the Digital Age

You're going through a breakup. You've realized that, while you were in this relationship, you neglected nurturing relationships with a lot of your friends. You sit there, scrolling on social media. You haven't posted in a long time. You post a quote about breakups. You get a like. You feel better. Your WhatsApp then pings with a message from a friend you haven't spoken to in eight months; they have seen your "pain" posted online. Your brain fills with dopamine, the feel-good hormone. This makes you feel better. Dopamine is addictive. It makes us feel great; it masks our pain. It numbs like a drug. You want more. You post again. The response feels good. You feel like you haven't been forgotten by the tribe.

MORE DISCONNECTED THAN EVER BEFORE

We are using technology as a distraction from our loneliness. This behavior is particularly dangerous for teenagers. In an interview, Simon Sinek describes how social media addiction can take us away from the real connection and sense of belonging-ing we so desperately need:

> We're allowing unfettered access to these dopa-mine-producing devices and media, basically it's becoming hardwired and what we're seeing as they're growing older, too [is that] many kids don't know how to form deep, meaningful relationships. Their words not mine. They will admit that many of their friend-ships are superficial. They will admit that they don't rely or count on their friends. Deep meaningful rela-tionships are not there because they never practiced the skillset...[36]

Simon's words are backed by research. In the 2018 Cigna Loneliness Index, a study that spanned twenty thousand Americans, Gen Z (those eighteen to twenty-two at the time) were the loneliest of all generations. They registered ten of the eleven feelings associated with loneliness, including feel-ing like people around them are not really with them. It's a hard truth, but we are emotionally disconnected while hav-ing more access to each other than ever before in our history. Susan Pinker, author of *The Village Effect: Why Face-to-Face Contact Matters*, writes: "Digital devices are great for sharing information, but not great at deepening human connection and a sense of belonging." Technology alone does not quench our thirst for the connection we are wired to need. We have been using our technology in a way that makes us feel sur-rounded by surface-level connections, the virtual equivalent of standing at a party looking at all the guests and still feeling hauntingly alone. My greatest salve during this pandemic has been seeing devices used to engage with those we love in a more meaningful way.

USING TECHNOLOGY TO EMPHASIZE OUR HUMANITY

I am a Xennial. This means I had an analog childhood and a digital adulthood. It means I still remember connecting with people without a phone. I remember when social media was MySpace—and I didn't even have an account there. I also remember the excitement when I got my first brick-like red Nokia in the early 2000s and saw text messages coming through. For someone who craved connection, my use of early social media, such as Facebook, was like a heroin addiction. Sending and receiving messages would send my heart racing, and not just when dating but also when getting them from platonic friends. There were years of emptiness where my cell phone became a priority.

I still remember the first year I started thinking in Facebook statuses; it was 2010. I would be in a situation, being with friends, and actively look for a quip, a quote, or a headline to post about. That was the moment I stopped being present. At the time, I dismissed this as my "creative radio brain" and that it was a blessing, that this was my job, and indeed it became my job. As a decade passed, the demands on radio presenters to "up their socials" and post on the station Facebook became assurance to me that all of this was a skill. Today it is a skill that people will even pay to be coached on. Most of my business still comes in through social media marketing. Maybe you found out about this very book because of social media. This is not to say social media doesn't have its merits, but it is how we use it that matters most.

BEING IN THE MOMENT

Almost a decade on, and I am sitting across from one of my good friends. He's newly single. Another girlfriend and I have taken him out for his birthday dinner. At some point in the conversation, he just starts picking up his phone and swiping dating apps. Right in front of us, while we are talking to him, averting our eye contact. He's in his late thirties. Just like me, he's a Xennial. I've known this person a long time and know he isn't inherently rude. We continue talking, and then again, any time he seems to glaze over, up comes the phone as if we, the in-person connections in front of him, celebrating him on his birthday, don't matter. I'm a little annoyed, I admit.

I think we get annoyed when we see behavior we don't like in ourselves mirrored in others. It reminded me of my time in Dubai when I was more interested in posting about what I was doing than enjoying the actual moment. When the engagement with my online following was more important to me than the people in front of me. Here, a decade on, this was karma. I was being what author James A. Roberts terms "phubbed," snubbed by someone else's phone.[37] Before speaking, I watch my friend and look at his body language from the view of a communications veteran. His head is down, his eye contact is nonexistent, and his shoulders are overturned. Did the phone make him look like he had lost confidence, or was he actually not feeling good right now? When we are hunched over while using our phone, it gives off what author and communications expert Vanessa Van Edwards calls "loser" body language. The inward-facing rolled shoulders and the aversion to eye contact are in themselves blocking any opportunity for in-person, serendipitous connection.[38] "Loser" body language says, "Don't connect with me; I'm busy," to any passerby, the same way crossing your arms in front of you does.

"Are you okay?" my other friend and I both ask. He looks up and then spews a diatribe about how all the online dates were terrifying. I know the deep intimate loneliness that comes from seeing everyone else settling down. I was single for eight years. I know the deep pit-of-my-stomach, watering-of-the-eyes-inducing feeling of being hopeful about someone and then the rejection. For human beings, there are few things we fear more than the pain of rejection. We equate that lack of belonging as meaning we are cast out of the tribe.

What's scary now, though, is, where we once sat with this pain, we now turn to our phone to numb. Like my friend, I wanted to keep swiping until the pain of rejection could be replaced by the excitement of opportunity. A possible new person that may fill the void of not belonging and make me feel safe. I would argue that we live in a world where there is so much ease of access to connections that three dates of something possibly authentic not working out can leave us feeling much more wounded than in that analog childhood of mine. This is for two reasons:

OPTIONITIS

In my view, we feel more easily wounded than before for two paradoxical reasons. The first is that we perceive we have both seen a glimpse of everything that is out there, but then at the same time, we have to keep moving and searching to find better options because the world has gotten more and more connected. For example, we can scan and swipe through a small city like Singapore's single population within an hour at a dinner table, and when the right profile doesn't present itself, this gives us the perception that there is truly no one out there for us.

The other side of the paradox, which also makes us feel really alone, is our belief that there is always someone or something better out there. Without the internet giving us access to new connections anywhere in the world, our ancestors would date village to village, maybe village to city if they felt adventurous, but certainly, there was no clicking on Facebook to find the love of your life living thousands of kilometers away. We are now faced with "optionitis," the perception that our intended soul mate could be anyone in seven billion people on the planet. Now, because of the internet, many people feel a sense of obligation to find that person and not spend their lives with just "any old person" we may have gone to high school with. I believe this overwhelming idea of options is yet another factor making us feel lonelier than ever. How can we possibly be mindful and present with what is in front of us when there is so much more to see?

This is because it means going wide instead of deep if you wanted to connect with as many people as possible. Our use of apps is advocating for shallower and faster romantic inter-actions in the hope of getting to meet someone better. This goes for dating but also networking and communicating with our existing connections. Chasing and searching for some-thing better is leaving us breathless, and it's leaving us sitting at our birthday dinner, not making eye contact with the actual people who love us, who are in front of us, who want to con-nect with us. It has made us less present.

I lived this for years, so no judgment on anyone. I can speak life into it because for eight years of singledom, as dating apps had just emerged, I experienced the frenetic energy of it all. It wasn't until after therapy that I quickly learned a lot of the time I could have spent on healing was spent on swiping.

DEEPER CONNECTIONS

Ten years ago, clicking into my Facebook was like looking at photographic proof of my "cool Dubai life." A world away from the messy suburban house in Perth ringing with my mother's shouting. If my life looks like this now, I thought, if I have manifested THIS, then I am safe from ever having to go back to living THAT life. Here I am loved. On this curated page of my own values circulating with the values and lifestyles of my friends who look just like me, I am safe. This means I am not crazy and unlovable, there are people just like me, and they are my tribe, even if we have never really spoken to each other with any depth.

This farce came crashing down when I went back to Perth when Mom had her stroke. Those wide, shallow connections will never hold you in grief. I needed to look up from my phone at the people who really cared about me. The ones who dropped flowers at my door on my birthday. The ones who brought me soup and food when I was single and ill and knew that I couldn't cook for myself. The ones who I could be vulnerable with. These are the markers of authentic connections. I would argue we all need to look up from our phones more. Put the damn things away sometimes. I think we are on the edge of a mass awakening where people are craving time away from their devices. Maybe that's one of the gifts of the pandemic and its tech burnout. Many of us have just had enough of being held hostage by our phones.

Your device, however, is not the villain. It doesn't have to be all or nothing with technology. Technology has an incredible propensity to connect us, as we've seen with the pandemic, but this is only if it's used correctly. I am a huge proponent of using technology to spread not just the message of human connection but also doing the connecting itself. Here's what social media and smartphones can give us in the way of connection.

USE TECHNOLOGY TO ENHANCE YOUR LIFE, NOT DISTRACT FROM IT

When I was nineteen and my father was dying of cancer, we did not have smartphones. My mother's rare degenerative disease (which is literally eroding tissue in her brain as we speak) means her short-term memory is fast disappearing. Five years ago, she forgot the days of the week and the times of the day. Three years ago, she forgot my father died in 2004, and in 2018, the doctors said she would pass. She has not. Like all good, overbearing Asian mothers, maybe she is holding on to see me get married.

When I heard this news in 2018, my reaction was probably not what most people experience. I started filming my mother and documenting what I believed to be our last lucid moments together via social media and my phone. This was all because I don't have video of my dad from 2004 because we didn't have smartphones then. Anyone who has experienced profound personal loss knows that photos only give us so much. Over time, I have forgotten his mannerisms, the tone of his voice, and his smile. I was not about to let that happen to me for the second time, so I began recording my mother.

I began capturing so many moments with her in Perth on my visits and rewatching them when I returned to Singapore, reminding myself of our love. Studies show that the simple act of watching a video of people we love can elicit the social bonding hormone oxytocin and make us feel a lot better. Video has blessed us with far more emotional information to connect with than still images, voice notes, or text messages.

After my mother had her stroke, she forgot her Facebook password. In 2020, on her birthday during the global lockdown, I was hit with a wave of sadness as her dormant Facebook account, still connected with mine, reminded me: "Today is Sandra Heng's Birthday." A small cake with candles animation blinked at me in the top right-hand corner of my Facebook profile. That Facebook account had reassured her that I was healthy and safe when I was in Dubai. She had made friends with my friends. She had gotten to see what the

Middle East looked like through my eyes. Then the lights went out. We tried to get her password back, but the disease beat us during the process. Her condition deteriorated so quickly that she can now no longer remember to even charge her phone.

Despite this, social media is still being used in my mom's life. During the worst of Australia's COVID-19 shutdown, social media inadvertently became her lifeline to the outside world once more. If used with intention, technology can soothe those in the most isolated of situations.

HUMAN CONNECTION SUPERHERO

My mother had been a teacher at Singapore's most elite girls school. She had regaled me and my sister with stories of her phenomenally high-achieving students. These women were Singapore's brightest and best, a nation whose education system is nothing to be laughed at. "They wrote entire essays in poetry," my mother would beam at us as kids, hoping the comparison would be made clear to us. Even though she taught there forty years ago, it's still a huge part of her identity. She retains the memories of this time because they are long-term memories; in effect, this part of her identity is how she remembers herself.

After I posted a video of Mom for her birthday on my Instagram, the school reshared it on their alumni page. The next morning, the day after my mother's seventy-second birthday, I woke up to these stories of connection. My mother at her best, like my father, the original Human Connection Superhero. Here are just some of the comments:

- "Mrs. Heng—Happy Birthday! You showed by example that we ladies can be anything we want to be. We borrowed your courage when we had little of it and grew into our own. I remember the time you confronted the flasher at the overhead bridge in Mrs. Sandra Heng style. And not only did you remove our fear but your empowered us to turn those situations around. After this COVID-19 situation, I will visit you in Perth. Stay beautiful and strong always!"

- "Happy Birthday, Mrs. Heng! I caught up with her about twelve years ago when I was in Perth."

- "Wow, she still speaks the same, her voice, diction, and mannerisms are the same since she was my Sec 2 Literature teacher in 1968. The last our cohort of 1970 caught up with her was during our thirty years anniversary in 2000. She was so sweet to fly down from Perth just for us."

- "Happy Birthday, Mrs. Heng. You taught us history in Sec 2/3 in 1970. A real inspiration to all of us. Great teacher and beautiful. May God bless you every moment."

I called my mother immediately; I knew this would be the best gift for her self-described "lonely heart." As I read the messages to her, she sobbed. She felt remembered, acknowledged, and CONNECTED once again to the community beyond the walls of that nursing home, just as she had once empowered the voice of each of these young women and made *them* feel acknowledged.

There are a few things we can learn from this story about using technology to bolster our human connection. Firstly, this incident had an incredible connective and emotional impact on the women she taught. The connection spanned two continents, Asia and Australia, yet not one person met face-to-face during this story. It involved social media platforms and a phone call used in the right way to give a healthy dose of oxytocin and dopamine to all involved. This is just one of many examples of how we can diminish loneliness for people we love using our devices.

Secondly, as a result of this interplay of technology, as you can see in the comments Mom received, some of the ladies will be flying to visit her. So using technology to create face-to-face human connection should be the aim. Lastly, like a happy marriage, technology and human connection should encourage and support each other. The digital should, however, always take a secondary role to face-to-face.

Dr. John Cacioppo from the University of Chicago clarifies it further by saying, "If you use those [digital] connections as a way station—it's associated with lower levels of loneliness. If it's used as a destination—and ironically, lonely people tend to do this, they tend to withdraw socially because it's punishing, and interacting digitally perhaps as a non-authentic self, makes them feel more like they're accepted. But it doesn't actually make them feel less lonely."

One of my final points on using technology to make us feel more connected is that, as Dr. Cacioppo mentions, we should be using it to show up as our authentic selves. Using it not as a highlight reel as I did in my twenties but as means of expressing our true values, beliefs, and vulnerabilities. Only then does it attract and connect us to others.

USE VOICE NOTES TO AUGMENT YOUR HUMANITY.

Almost all social media apps now have the ability to send voice notes as a direct message.

Your voice has the power to change the life of someone on the edge. Communication isn't actually about you; it's about the person you are trying to connect with. Give them the gift of hearing your voice and hearing how much you care. How could you better use the voice note feature on your social media and messaging apps? Try sending voice notes more often.

Here's an example of this that occurred during the chaos of our March 2020 lockdown in Singapore. A local food delivery driver went viral when, amid the fear and grave uncertainty of the pandemic, he sent his waiting customer fully produced voice notes at 5:00 a.m. to update her on the status of her food delivery. He provided human connection at a time when people were anxious and thirsty for it, and the story soothed us all. The voice notes were kind and warm, but they also had music performed by Yiruma behind them. Where drivers would normally allow automated text messages to update a client instead, Arif, the delivery driver, showed us a human was behind the service.

BE A PRESENT FRIEND.

A year ago, I started preshooting and batch-banking all of my social media content so that when I was connecting with people in person, I was fully present. I decided to take images of my life only when it is a special occasion, not if I am just doing a normal weekday catch-up with someone I love. I chose not to interrupt the flow of conversation to take pictures or videos of us together or our meals. Instead, I focus on being there and being fully engaged, leaning into those incredible, everyday moments of connection. It is the best way I have found to be present while still meeting the social media marketing demands of my speaking business. How could you create your own boundaries with your social media use that work for you?

SET LIMITS ON SCROLLING.

We all know by now the mental health implications of scrolling too much and how the comparison trap can rob us of our gratitude. I love the creativity of making content. It's what I know how to do, but I don't scroll very often. I reply to comments underneath my posts but don't go down the rabbit hole of scrolling my day away. Are you scrolling too much? How could you create a boundary for scrolling that works uniquely for you? Remember, most of us compare the messy back end of our lives to the highlight reel someone else posts of theirs. It's not real, and it's not worth your mental health.

MAKE EYE CONTACT WHENEVER POSSIBLE.

Eye contact has got to be one of the most important things in using technology in an era where we are experiencing social distancing. It's important to remember that direct eye contact allows people to trust us more, and without trust, there is no connection. Human beings are skeptical of people who do not look us in the eye. When using virtual conferencing for work, put your camera on, direct your gaze to the small camera on the top of your laptop, and engage with the audience viewing you on the other side. An added tip, should this feel weird or uncomfortable for you, is to imagine the person you love the most in the entire world is behind the camera. This will engage a warmth in your eyes that primes you for connection and dispels the "deer in the headlights" look we get when we do something uncomfortable.

CONCLUSION

At the time of writing this, my mother turns seventy-four in three days. Last night I opened my email with glee as my G2G pass to enter Australia was approved. Since COVID-19, Perth had become a bastion of pandemic-freeness and normalcy. People are basking on beaches maskless, and the government wants to keep it that way. So, I applied for the pass, putting "sick relative" as my travel exemption reason. They asked me, "What are your plans for your travel within Australia?" I type nervously, having already been denied entry once:

> I will fly and stay only in the metropolitan area. After arrival, I will quarantine for two weeks in a government-approved quarantine hotel. I will then go to my local doctor for an Australian 2020 flu vaccine so I can enter the nursing home. I will visit my mother for the one week I am there. I will be staying with an aunt and will also visit my godchildren. Then I will return to Singapore.

With its crazy overpriced ticket and its longer time spent

in quarantine than on the ground, this trip is ridiculous, but it is, like most irrational things, based on love. Deep oceans of love that I have for my mother. There is no one else in the world I would do this for.

When they ask me to explain my reason for visiting, I want to say, "Filial piety." Can I put "love"? Instead, I write pleadingly to be allowed in:

> My mother has a rare degenerative illness; I have not seen her since December 2019. At any moment, she could have a life-ending stroke. I would not forgive myself if this happened, and I haven't seen her for so long.

It's stark to be forced to write your anxiety down in this desperate way. The melodrama of it. Maybe Mrs. M was right all those years ago in English class because it is highly likely an automated system is scanning my form. Yet, how can it be dramatic or exaggerated when it is the truth? Black-and-white print on a form with a flashing cursor brings the situation into stark relief. Since 2013, I have been on tenterhooks thinking about the sudden stroke that could take her from us forever.

CONNECTION IS LOVE

The largest part of my healing was not just forgiving my mother but learning who she was in her entirety. Researching who she was before I was born for this book and seeing everything she went through justified so many of her actions. She was ill and didn't know it; she was new in a foreign country, had no internet, and had her own wounds from her own childhood. We often resent our parents for the things they did to hurt us, but that resentment is not something you want to have in your heart when they pass. I am so much of her that to resent her would be to resent myself. It took years, and sometimes it is still very stressful connecting with her, but I have come to realize that I love her deeply despite it all and because of it all.

I am not the only one who loves my mother deeply, who was wrapped up in her fierce charisma. I know this because when I returned to live in Singapore in 2015, I was inundated by emails to my website and social media asking me if I was indeed Sandra Heng's daughter and then questions from her former students on how they could get in touch with her. These girls have now grown into community leaders; they are busy women. They must have seen me on TV, I thought. For all my wanting to put oceans between my mother and me and unlearn her programming, I still wore her on my face. I look just like a Chinese version of my mom.

Upon replying to these direct messages, these women called my mother to speak to her. Those still profoundly touched by her mentoring flew four thousand kilometers to her nursing home in Australia to sit by her side. They bought my mother designer watches and scarves as if they were her own daughters.

STOLEN MEMORIES

For my first paid speech on International Women's Day in 2018, I didn't know any prominent female businesswomen personally to profile, which is what the client wanted. So, I called my mom up in the nursing home, and I asked her for the names of some of her former students so I could research them for the piece. She sat there clutching the phone in her remaining good arm, hunched with her breasts touching the waistband of her diapers.

"Mama, can you tell me the name of the student you had who was the engineer on the Singapore train system?"

My mom pauses. "Simone, I am just so proud of them."

"I know you're proud, Mom, but I need some names. What about the woman who was the CFO of that bank?"

My mom pauses a little longer. "Simone, I am just so proud of them."

"Right, Mom, I know you're proud, but I really, really need names for my speech. What about the surgeon, the one that was a member of MENSA?"

I am almost rolling my eyes now. I am getting impatient.

This time my mother pauses for an inordinate amount of time.

"Simone, I am just so proud of them." Her voice breaks. A pause. My eyes water because I realize she is ashamed because she cannot remember their names.

This story yields our final three takeaways on genuine, lifelong human connection. The details of your achievements, what job title you have, or how much money you earn—in the end, those material accouterments are so unimportant. My mother couldn't remember anyone by their job title. What she remembers and what matters, as Maya Angelou said, was how those students "made her feel."

My mother remembers the pride she felt for these girls and the inspiration they gave her in teaching them. There is an equal energetic exchange that comes with true connection. And that brings me to the second takeaway from this story: reciprocity.

CONNECTION, RECIPROCITY, AND CONSISTENCY

How can we tell a connection is authentic? Authentic human connection, to me, is reciprocal. The same way my mother was lit up inside by the experience of teaching these young girls, they were forever changed by the experience of being taught by her. Just as she never stopped feeling proud of them, they never forgot how she inspired them. So much so that these busy women would fly four thousand kilometers to sit with her in a nursing home on their annual leave forty years later.

In 2019, I had tea with some of her former students in a huge house in Bukit Timah, and photo albums were piled high onto the table. I saw my mother, much prettier than I, skinny-legged like Twiggy. In shift dresses and large glasses with short, curly hair. I often wondered what my mother had done to them to make them feel so connected to her. The answer is that she mentored them the way she parented me. She went beyond the student–teacher relationship. Their words:

- "She asked us our opinion on things she wanted to buy for her home."

- "She invited the whole class to her new flat she bought with your dad. There she taught us to bake a pineapple upside-down cake."

- "She was fierce, but we knew she cared. She'd sit on her desk holding a ball of string threatening to tie our legs together if we didn't cross them like ladies."

"Sounds like my mom," I said, concealing my pride. Concealing my wonder actually because I had always thought her to be nicer to them than us. She was the same. She was consistent. Consistency builds trust. So if we want to build powerful connection, we have to put in the energy to show up consistently for people we love over the long haul.

The third and final point is that human connection rests on our humanity. To approach people not through the lens of their occupation or with an agenda, but simply as our fellow tribesmen. You are human before you are any of the labels the world puts on you, from your job title to your roles as mother or daughter, for example. She went beyond the student–teacher relationship to care for and mentor these girls.

HUMAN CONNECTIONS ARE OUR LEGACY

When you're alone at the end of your life, your children grown up, how you will be remembered will be dictated by the seeds of human connection you have sown in your life. Your human connections are your legacy.

Human connection is at the center of almost everything we do; it is how we are wired, and a lack of it is the foundation for mental health issues like addiction, depression, and hoarding that we are seeing soar today. The postpandemic years will see a level of social awkwardness, a mental health crisis, and hopefully, a recalibration of our use of technology. But by drawing attention to the topic of human connection, it is my hope we can get better at it and be more resilient to these issues. In very plain language, if you want to be happy and live at the highest expression of yourself, you need healthy human connection.

We also need love and belonging to grow into the best versions of ourselves, and the wounds from our childhood affect how we love and build relationships with others as adults. It's up to us to be courageous and reconnect with ourselves. The opposite of courage in this would be to numb our pain. We can develop addictions when we soothe the pain of disconnection with behaviors like sex, drugs, alcohol, social media use, work, and more.

Sometimes the only way to overcome this disconnection is to be humbled and apologize. I have done it many times, and

I have been happier as a result. It has allowed me to move on with my life and invest fully in my new relationships.

In these new relationships, service should be at the center of how we communicate and love. An others-driven approach builds rapport and authenticity in our connections. Part of the authenticity also comes from unplugging from how we have been taught to show emotion. By expressing our emotions more fully in our words, in our bodies, and on our faces. Remember, when we show transparency, this tells others we are safe to connect with.

Remember that quality over quantity is the best approach when making new connections. Cultivate depth as opposed to a large superficial network. We can also help by looking at the lives of expatriates, following their cues for bravely putting themselves out there to meet new people, and learning to scan for commonalities when connecting in our highly polarized world.

Technology is not going away; it is going to be a huge part of our future and how we connect. We can use it as the next best thing to face-to-face connection, or we can abuse it. Face-to-face, in-person connection still trumps all other modalities. Connecting with people is the most valuable skill you can have in an era when people are thirsty for connection.

If anything in this book connected with you, please let me know. I collect stories of connection from around the world. You can email me through my website www.simoneheng.com with anything you want to share. If this book has brought you to the precipice of understanding more about yourself, and this self-connection has prompted you to want to speak to a professional, I'd be happy to connect you with a great therapist.

Lastly, I am on almost all different kinds of social media and use the DMs to engage in heartfelt voice note conversations on this topic of human connection with many. Please feel free to find me @simoneheng on Instagram or SimoneHeng-Speaker on LinkedIn. Let's connect!

ACKNOWLEDGMENTS

To the Scribe team. The time difference was not easy, but it was so worth it. I would never have been able to achieve this dream of writing my first book without your help. Thank you for everything.

Thank you to the wonderful thought leaders and authors who gave their time to blurb this book. Shadé Zahrai, Sue Cheung, Steve Sims, and Shelly Tygielski. You were so busy with your own projects yet made time to help me. That is genuine human connection through service.

Thank you to the interviewees who gave their time and allowed their stories to be featured. I literally could not have done this without you. Dr. James Coan, Shelly Tygielski, Helen, Heather, Viv, Kanitha, and Christina. I am so grateful to you.

Thank you to the staff of my mother's nursing home facility. I am continuously in awe of your patience and your heart. Each of you is a living saint who has inspired many of the themes of this book. Thanks for making the winter of Mom's life the best it can be. I would not be able to tell these stories without knowing she is being cared for all those thousands of miles away.

To the late Cameron Plant. I miss you every day. Thank you for being an exceptional human connector. Your story, in part, inspired me to write this book.

To Aunty Vicky and Uncle Muralee. Thank you for being my surrogate parents and helping my shrinking family when you had so much to deal with on your own. Thank you for giving me the space to learn who my parents were before I knew them and giving me the grace to process it all through conversation and a cup of tea at your kitchen table.

To Paula, my best friend. There are no words big enough to thank you for being with me on life's journey. There were years and years where I had no one except for you. Thank you for being the absolute ground zero of trust where I can say anything. Thank you for telling me to seek professional help in the most loving way possible. There would be no thriving and certainly no book without your support.

To Paul. The man who allowed the writing time for this book to happen from 7:00–9:00 a.m. every morning for almost a year. You gave me a block of time every day, so I could simply be with my manuscript, taking the dogs out so I could complete this project. I am so indebted to your love, generosity, and support. Thank you so much.

To my sister, Tamara. Thank you for being such a responsible sibling, so I could pursue such projects as this.

To my late father, Robert Heng, whose humility, grace, and kindness I try to emulate every day. You always knew how to treat people fairly, and you always put us first. I hope this book helps people see that there is such brilliance and wisdom in their local shopkeeper should they take a moment to truly connect with him. I could not have asked for a better father. Thank you.

To my beautiful mom, Sandra Heng. A lump rises in my throat just thinking how inadequate the words "thank you" are in acknowledging the contribution you have made to my life. What would I be without you; how much less would I have done in my life if not for your tough love? I know without a doubt that you did the best you could with what you had at the time. I hope this book and other projects I create help to keep the vibrant version of you in the world.

ABOUT THE AUTHOR

Simone Heng is a human connection specialist and former international broadcaster for the likes of Virgin Radio Dubai, HBO Asia, and CNBC, among others. With over fifteen years of experience as a communicator on air, on stage, and one-on-one in different countries, connection has always been her life's work.

As a speaker, Simone inspires people to connect in a world thirsty for connection. She has spoken to thousands and often for Fortune 500 organizations. Her clients include Google, Bytedance, Salesforce, SAP, L'Oréal, TEDx, the United Nations, and many more. Simone and her work have been featured on CNN and in *Vogue, Elle,* and *Harper's Bazaar,* among others.

Simone is based and was born in Singapore but has also studied in Switzerland, was raised in Australia, and worked in the United Arab Emirates. She has a communications and cultural studies degree from Curtin University of Technology.

Secret Pandemic: The Search for Connection in a Lonely World is her first book.

ENDNOTES

1 Tim Sitt, "What is Self-Connection?" *The Freedom to Move Group*, December 21, 2018, https://www.freedomtomovegroup.com/blog-1/what-is-self-connection.

2 "Cigna 2018 U.S. Loneliness Index," Cigna, https://www.cigna.com/assets/docs/newsroom/loneliness-survey-2018-updated-fact-sheet.pdf.

3 Kira Asatryan, "4 Disorders That May Thrive on Loneliness," *Psychology Today*, July 23, 2015, https://www.psychologytoday.com/us/blog/the-art-closeness/201507/4-disorders-may-thrive-loneliness; Jed Diamond, "Loneliness: The Hidden Problem at the Root of Male Irritability, Anger, and Violence," *The Willits News*, December 14, 2020, https://www.willitsnews.com/2020/12/14/loneliness-the-hidden-problem-at-the-root-of-male-irritability-anger-and-violence.

4 Andrew Curry, "Ancient Bones Offer Clues to How Long Ago Humans Cared for the Vulnerable," *NPR*, June 17, 2020, https://www.npr.org/sections/goatsandsoda/2020/06/17/878896381/ancient-bones-offer-clues-to-how-long-ago-humans-cared-for-the-vulnerable.

5 Johann Hari, *Lost Connections: Why You're Depressed and How to Find Hope* (London: Bloomsbury, 2018).

6 Matthew D. Lieberman, *Social: Why Our Brains Are Wired To Be Social* (New York: Crown, 2013).

7 "Loneliness Is Bad for Your Health," *Association for Psychological Science*, August 17, 2007, https://www.psychologicalscience.org/news/releases/loneliness-is-bad-for-your-health.html.

8 Brett McKay, "Podcast #618: Finding Connection in a Lonely World," June 10, 2020, in *The Art of Manliness*, podcast, https://www.artofmanliness.com/people/relationships/connection-in-a-lonely-world-vivek-murthy.

9 William Shaw et al., "Stress Effects on the Body," *American Psychological Association*, November 1, 2018, https://www.apa.org/topics/stress/body.

10 Eric Klinenberg, "Is Loneliness a Health Epidemic?" *The New York Times*, February 9, 2018, https://www.nytimes.com/2018/02/09/opinion/sunday/loneliness-health.html.

11 Saul McLeod, "Maslow's Hierarchy of Needs," *Simply Psychology*, last modified December 29, 2020, https://www.simplypsychology.org/maslow.html.

12 "Study Reveals Locked-down People Favoured 'Old School Tech' during Coronavirus Pandemic," *The Hindu*, March 9, 2021, https://www.thehindu.com/society/connecting-during-covid19-natalie-pennington-study-technology/article34017230.ece.

13 "The Gifts Hub," Brené Brown, accessed August 12, 2021, https://brenebrown.com/thegifts-hub.

14 Karen D. Rudolph, Melissa S. Caldwell, and Colleen S. Conley, "Need for Approval and Children's Well-Being," *Child Development* 76, no. 2 (March 2005): 309–23, https://dx.doi.org/10.1111%2Fj.1467-8624.2005.00847_a.x.

15 Stephanie Lee, "Beyond Drugs: The Universal Experience of Addiction," *Dr. Gabor Maté*, April 5, 2017, https://drgabormate.com/opioids-universal-experience-addiction.

16 Bruce D. Perry and Oprah Winfrey, *What Happened to You?: Conversations on Trauma, Resilience, and Healing* (New York: Flatiron Books, 2021).

17 Kim Parker, Juliana Menasce Horowitz, and Rachel Minkin, "How Coronavirus Has Changed the Way Americans Work," *Pew Research Center*, December 9, 2020, https://www.pewresearch.org/social-trends/2020/12/09/how-the-coronavirus-outbreak-has-and-hasnt-changed-the-way-americans-work.

18   Jane Kelly, "We Asked an Expert Why We Hold Hands, and Learned It's Good for You," *UVA Today*, February 13, 2020, https://news.virginia.edu/content/we-asked-expert-why-we-hold-hands-and-learned-its-good-you.

19   Robert Hudak, "Hoarding Disorder: DSM-5 Criteria, Clinical Features, Epidemiology, and Comorbidities," *Psychopharmacology Institute*, January 1, 2021, https://psychopharmacologyinstitute.com/section/hoarding-disorder-dsm-5-criteria-clinical-features-epidemiology-and-comorbidities-2576-4959.

20   Julianne Holt-Lunstad, Timothy B. Smith, and J. Bradley Layton, "Social Relationships and Mortality Risk: A Meta-Analytic Review," *PLoS Medicine*, July 27, 2010, https://doi.org/10.1371/journal.pmed.1000316.

21   "Learning How to Say 'I'm Sorry'," *Harvard Mental Health Letter* (March 2008): 4–5, https://annmacdonalddotnet.files.wordpress.com/2011/07/how-to-say-im-sorry.pdf.

22   "Learning How to Say 'I'm Sorry'."

23   Aaron Lazare, "Making Peace through Apology," *Greater Good Magazine*, September 1, 2004, https://greatergood.berkeley.edu/article/item/making_peace_through_apology.

24   Vanessa Van Edwards, "You Are Contagious," TEDx Talks, YouTube video, June 27, 2017, https://www.youtube.com/watch?v=cef35Fk7YD8.

25   Amy Cuddy, "Your Body Language May Shape Who You Are," TED Talks, June 2012, https://www.ted.com/talks/amy_cuddy_your_body_language_may_shape_who_you_are.

26   Tony Robbins, "How to Change Your Words, Change Your Life," Tony Robbins, accessed June 10, 2021, https://www.tonyrobbins.com/mind-meaning/change-your-words-change-your-life.

27   "Are There Universal Facial Expressions?" Paul Ekman Group, accessed June 30, 2020, https://www.paulekman.com/resources/universal-facial-expressions.

28   James A. Russell, "Is There Universal Recognition of Emotion from Facial Expression? A Review of the Cross-Cultural Studies," *Psychological Bulletin* 115, no. 1 (1994): 102–41, https://doi.org/10.1037/0033-2909.115.1.102.

29   Marco Marini et al., "The Impact of Facemasks on Emotion Recognition, Trust Attribution and Re-Identification," *Scientific Reports* 11, no. 1 (December 2021), https://doi.org/10.1038/s41598-021-84806-5.

30   "The Real Health Benefits of Smiling," SCL Health, accessed October 30, 2021, https://www.sclhealth.org/blog/2019/06/the-real-health-benefits-of-smiling-and-laughing.

31   Robert A. Lavine, "How Eye Contact Brings You Together (or Pulls You Apart)," *Psychology Today*, September 11, 2016, https://www.psychologytoday.com/us/blog/neuro-behavioral-betterment/201609/how-eye-contact-brings-you-together-or-pulls-you-apart.

32   Susan Pinker, "The Secret to Living Longer May Be Your Social Life," TED Talk, April 2017, https://www.ted.com/talks/susan_pinker_the_secret_to_living_longer_may_be_your_social_life.

33   Olga Khazan, "How Loneliness Makes You Worse at Social Interaction." *The Atlantic*, April 7, 2017, https://www.theatlantic.com/health/archive/2017/04/how-loneliness-begets-loneliness/521841.

34   "Dunbar's Number: Why We Can Only Maintain 150 Relationships." *BBC Future*, October 1, 2019, https://www.bbc.com/future/article/20191001-dunbars-number-why-we-can-only-maintain-150-relationships.

35   "Pandemic of Love," Shelly Tygielski, accessed October 30, 2021, https://www.shellytygielski.com/pandemic-of-love.

36   David Crossman, "Simon Sinek on Millennials in the Workplace," YouTube video, October 29, 2016, https://www.youtube.com/watch?v=hER0Qp6QJNU.

37   "Phubbing," Merriam-Webster, accessed October 30, 2021, https://www.merriam-webster.com/words-at-play/phubbing-words-we%27re-watching.

38   Vanessa Van Edwards, "The Power of Body Language," CreativeLive, accessed October 30, 2021, https://www.creativelive.com/class/power-body-language-vanessa-van-edwards.

Made in the USA
Las Vegas, NV
07 March 2024

86777798R10100